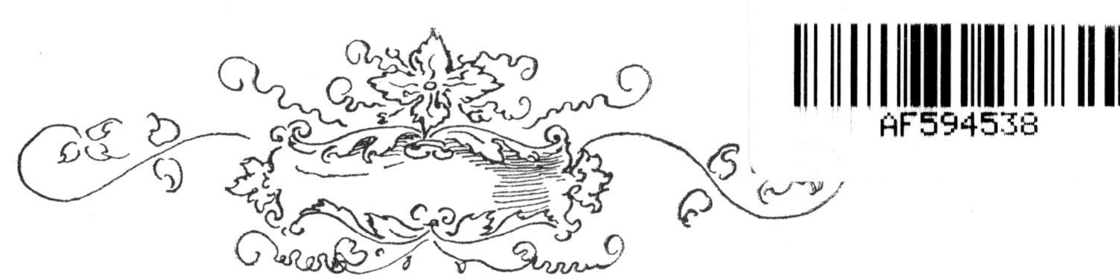

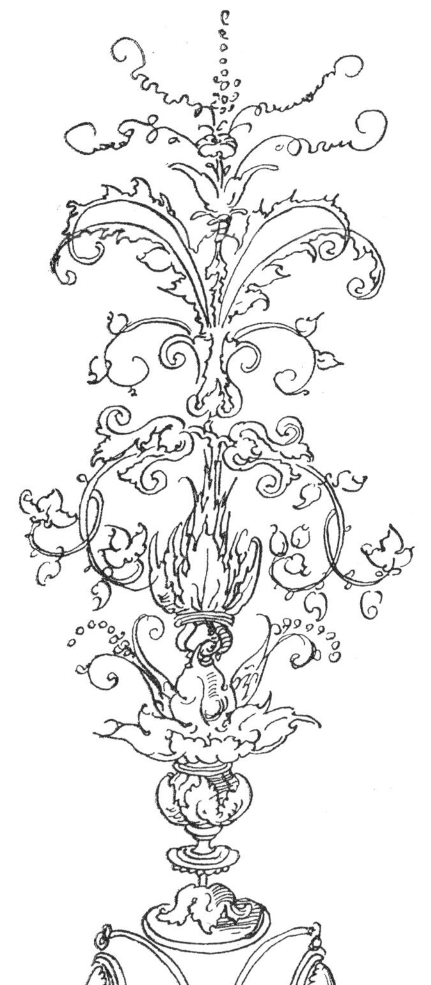

DÜRER'S DRAWINGS

FOR THE PRAYER-BOOK OF EMPEROR MAXIMILIAN I

53 PLATES

ALBRECHT DÜRER

DOVER PUBLICATIONS, INC.
MINEOLA, NEW YORK

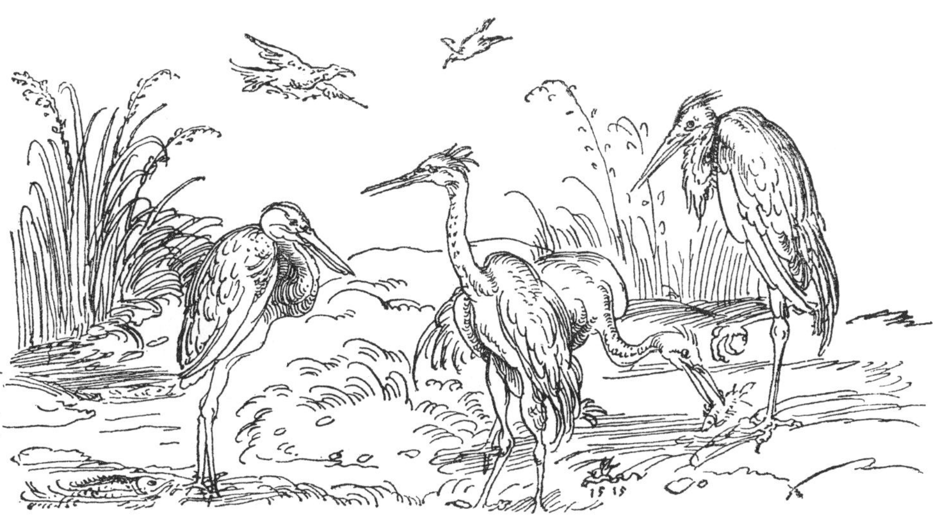

Copyright

Bibliographical Note

This Dover edition, first published in 2014, is an unabridged republication of *Albrecht Durer's Randzeichnungen zum Gebetbuche des Kaisers Maximilian I,* originally published in 1907 by G. Hirth's Kunstverlag, Munich. The preface and captions have been translated into English from the original German specially for this edition.

Library of Congress Cataloging-in-Publication Data

Dürer, Albrecht, 1471-1528.
[Drawings. Selections. English]
Dürer's drawings for the prayer-book of Emperor Maximilian I : 53 plates / Albrecht Dürer.
pages cm
Summary: "Holy Roman Emperor and King of the Germans Maximilian I was Albrecht Dürer's main patron from 1512 onward. These 45 pages of marginal drawings for the ruler's prayer book, unknown till their 1808 facsimile publication, reveal the artist's lighthearted and witty side. Includes 8 additional drawings by other artists." Provided by publisher.
"This Dover edition, first published in 2014, is an unabridged republication of Albrecht Dürer's Randzeichnungen zum Gebetbuche des Kaisers Maximilian I, originally published in 1907 by G. Hirth's Kunstverlag, Munich. The preface and captions have been translated into English from the original German specially for this edition."
ISBN-13: 978-0-486-49386-2 (pbk.)
ISBN-10: 0-486-49386-5
1. Prayer books—Illustrations. 2. Marginal illustrations. I. Title.
NC251.D8A4 2014
741.943--dc23
2013033990

Manufactured in the United States by Courier Corporation
49386501 2014
www.doverpublications.com

Preface to the First Edition

I will refrain from an explanation of these exquisite works and simply refer to what was said about them by Goethe at the beginning of this century, by Stöger and Lübke, and most recently by Thausing, Ephrussi, and Chmelarz.

I have left out the text of the prayer-book, for even if one can argue that simply "marginal drawings" are present here and a stylish reproduction must not only include the margins but also the body of every page, it is still beyond doubt that the enjoyment of Dürer's sublime fantasy creations is a greater one when we view them without the beautiful, though difficult and eye-tiring, Schonsperger font. The initials colored by a different hand act as an almost larger distraction. In as far as the drawings appear as allegories to the text, the following table of contents contains enough information. I for my part gladly forgo the discovery of questionable allegories where artistic expression itself captures it so perfectly. The beauty is beautiful even without the allegory.

The original drawings are known to be heavily faded. However, the light-sensitive photographic apparatus has, in a surprising way, conjured up contours and hatching marks from the old parchment that are no longer visible to the human eye.

The monograms and dates inscribed in black ink in the originals are apocryphal. However, it is professionally appropriate in the Dürer drawings. This is not so with the eight drawings by other hands, perhaps done by Lucas Cranach, or possibly also originating from a student or assistant of Dürer. Moritz Thausing suspected the hand of Hans Springinklee. Since the drawings, which are found in the continuation of the Besançon Prayer-Book and thought to have originated from the masters of Dürer's circle, are known through their publication in the yearbook of the art collections of the highest imperial family in Vienna, one can confidently claim that the last eight drawings of the Munich Prayer-Book, in artistic value, tower far above those in the Besançon Prayer-Book.

Table of Contents

The Drawings by Other Hands

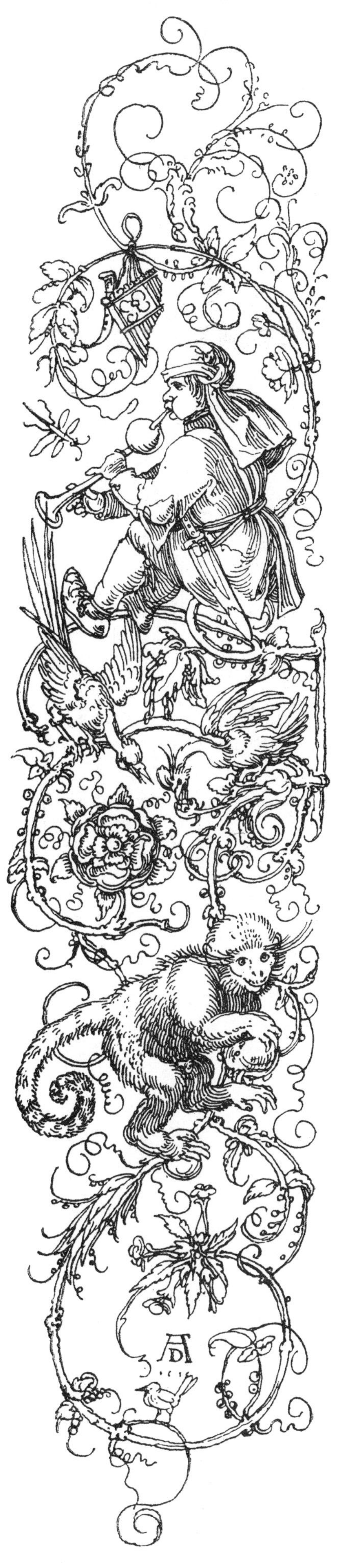

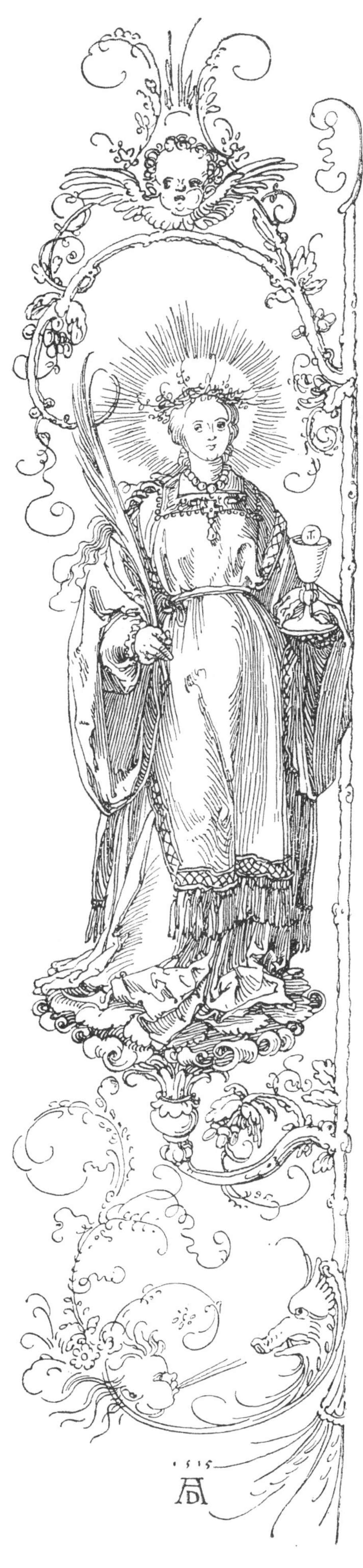

Plate 2

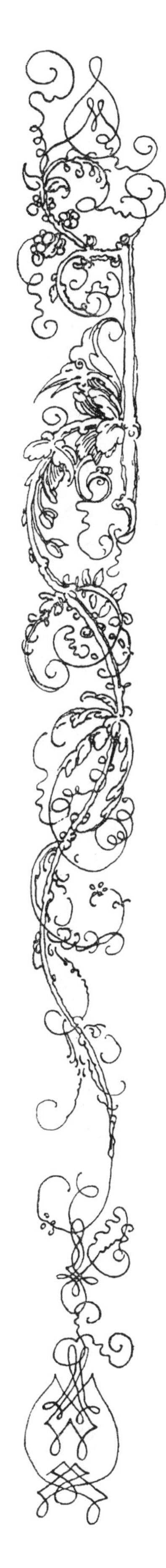

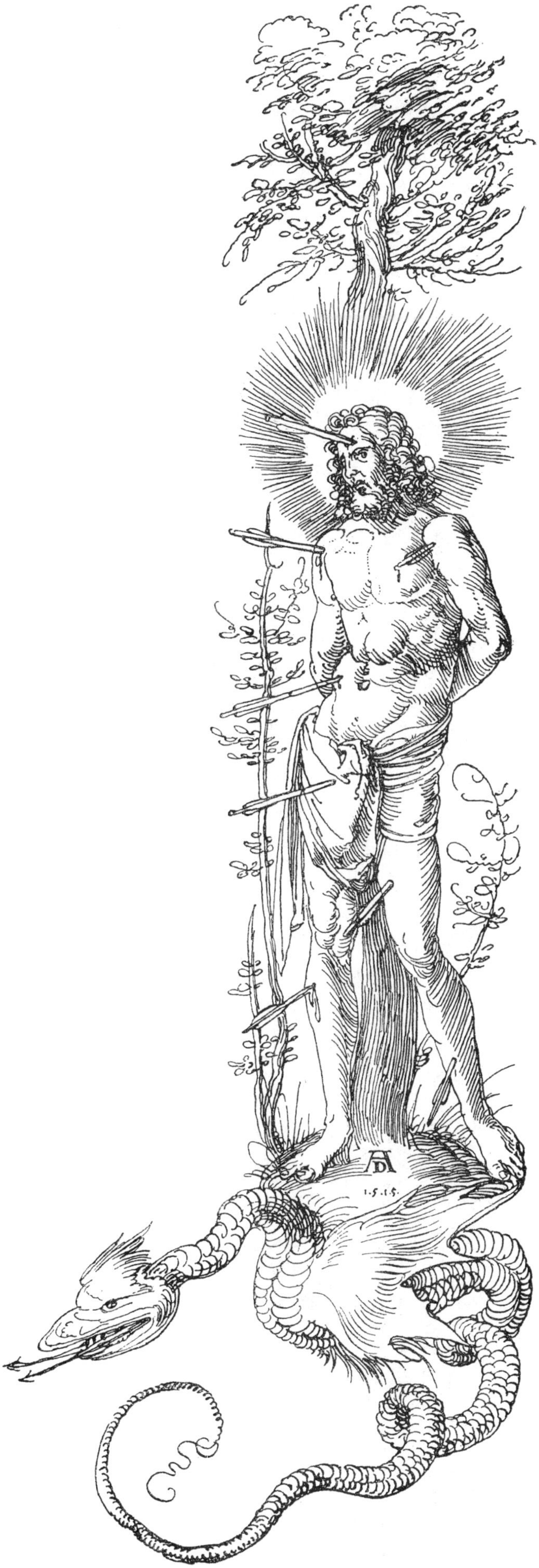

PLATE 3

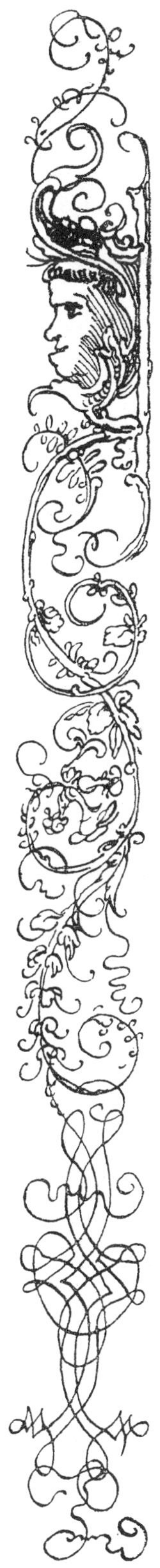

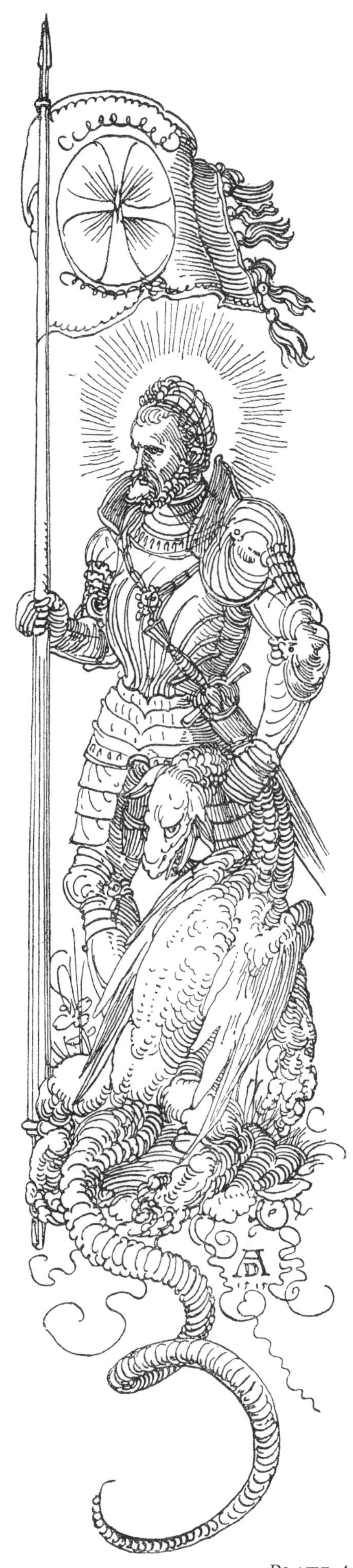

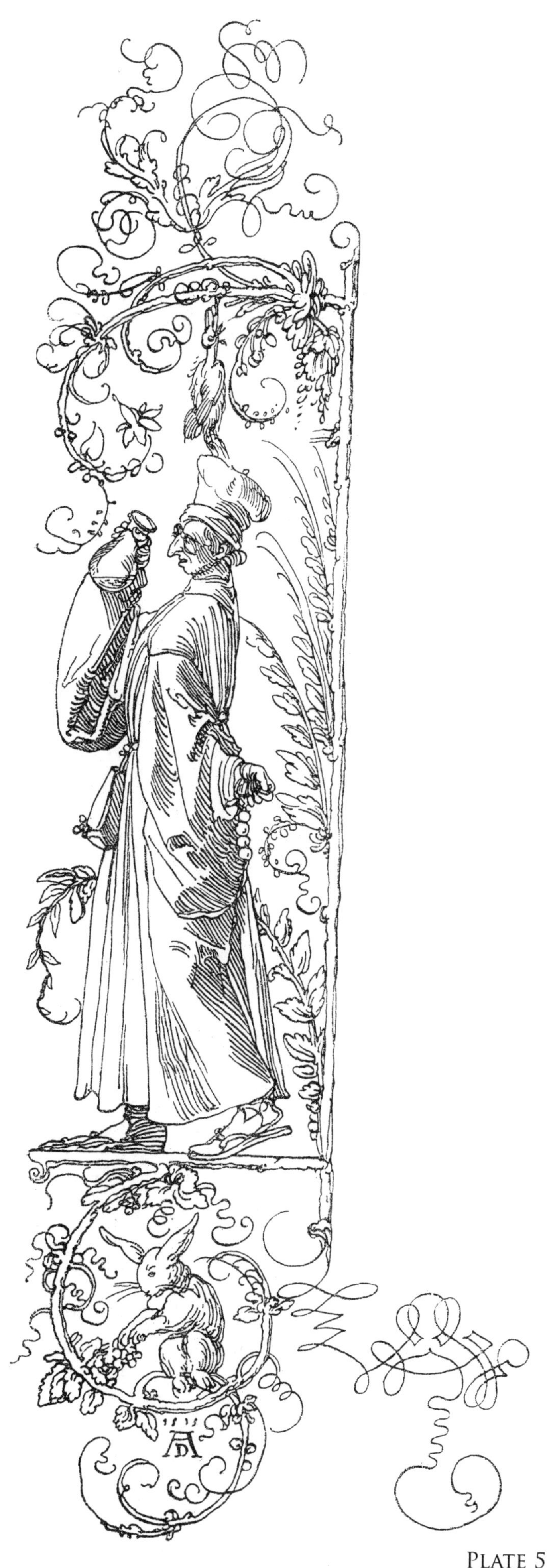

Plate 5

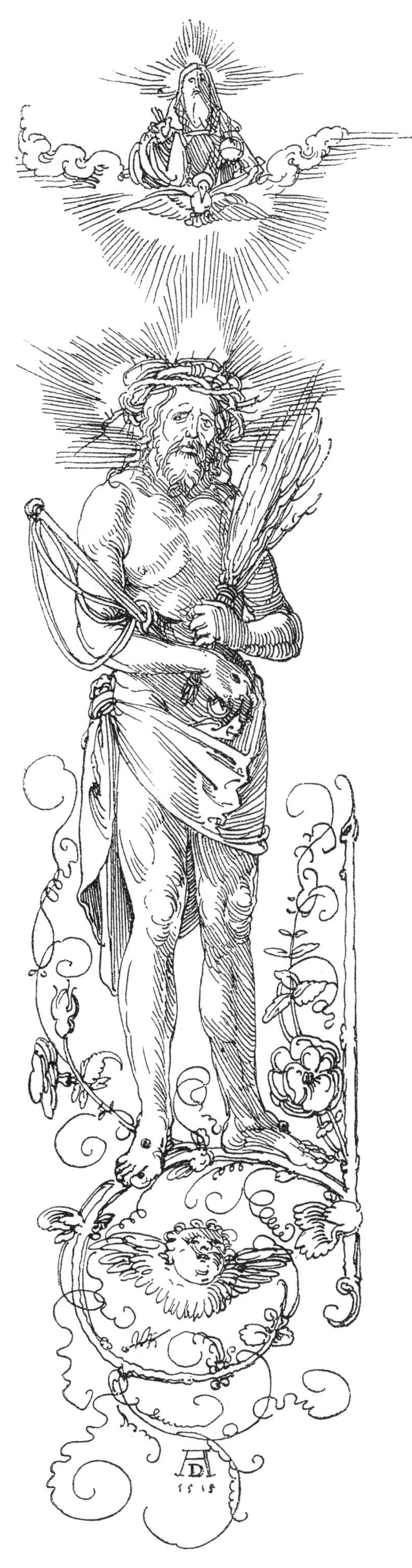

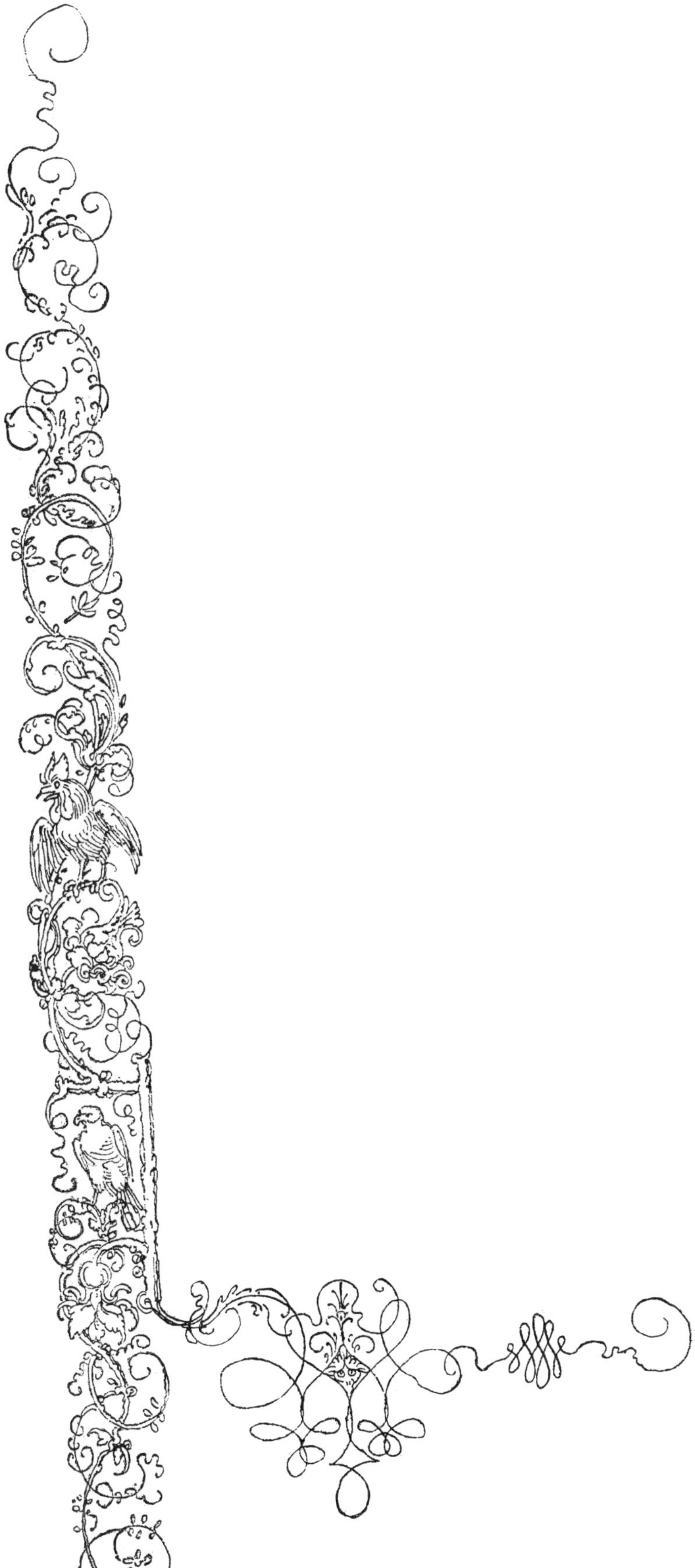

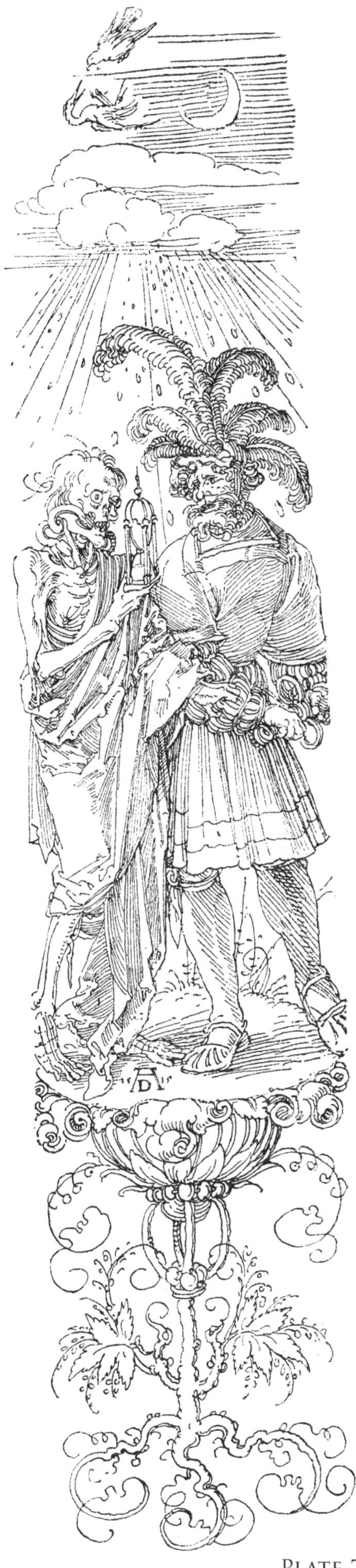

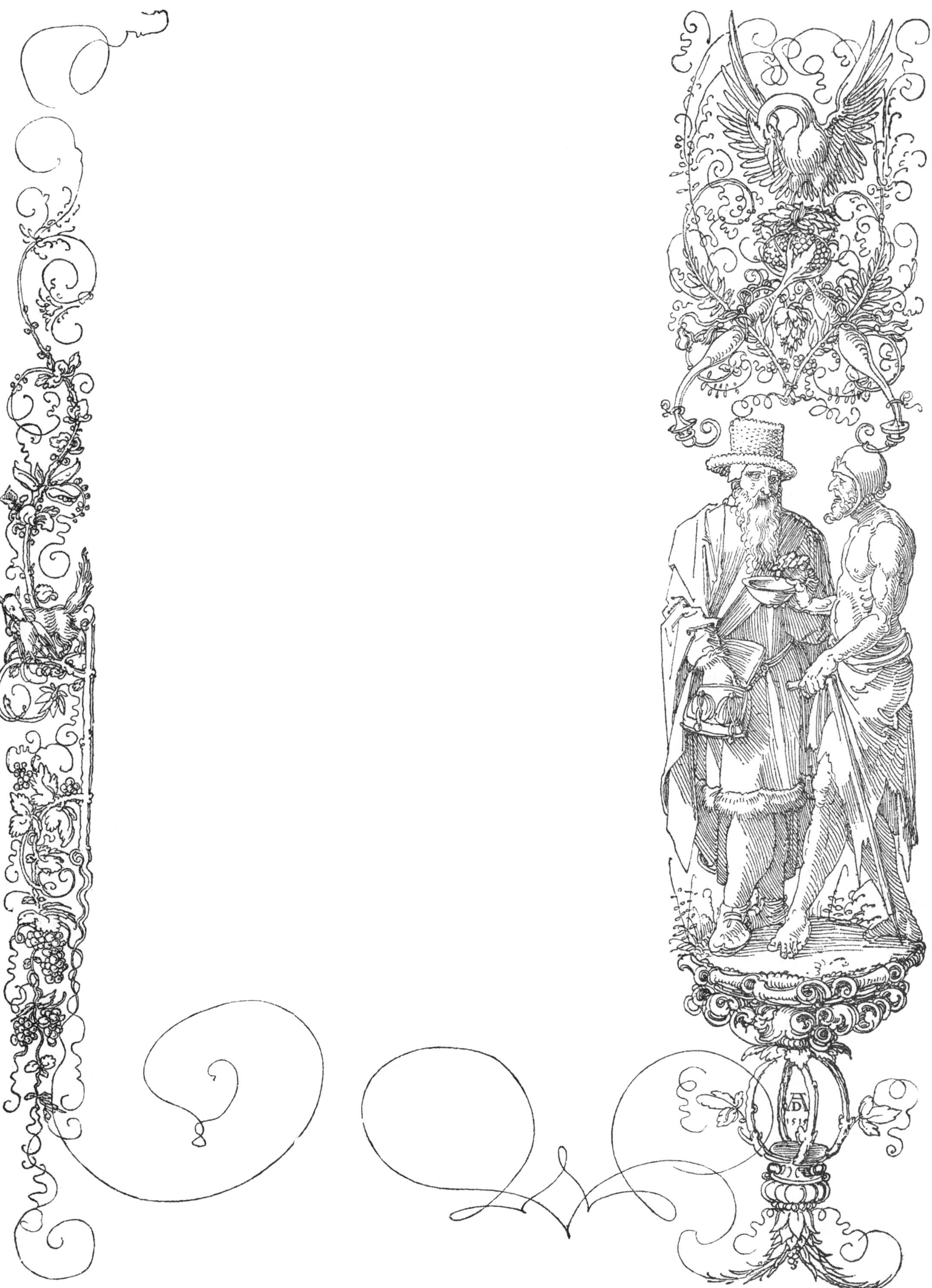

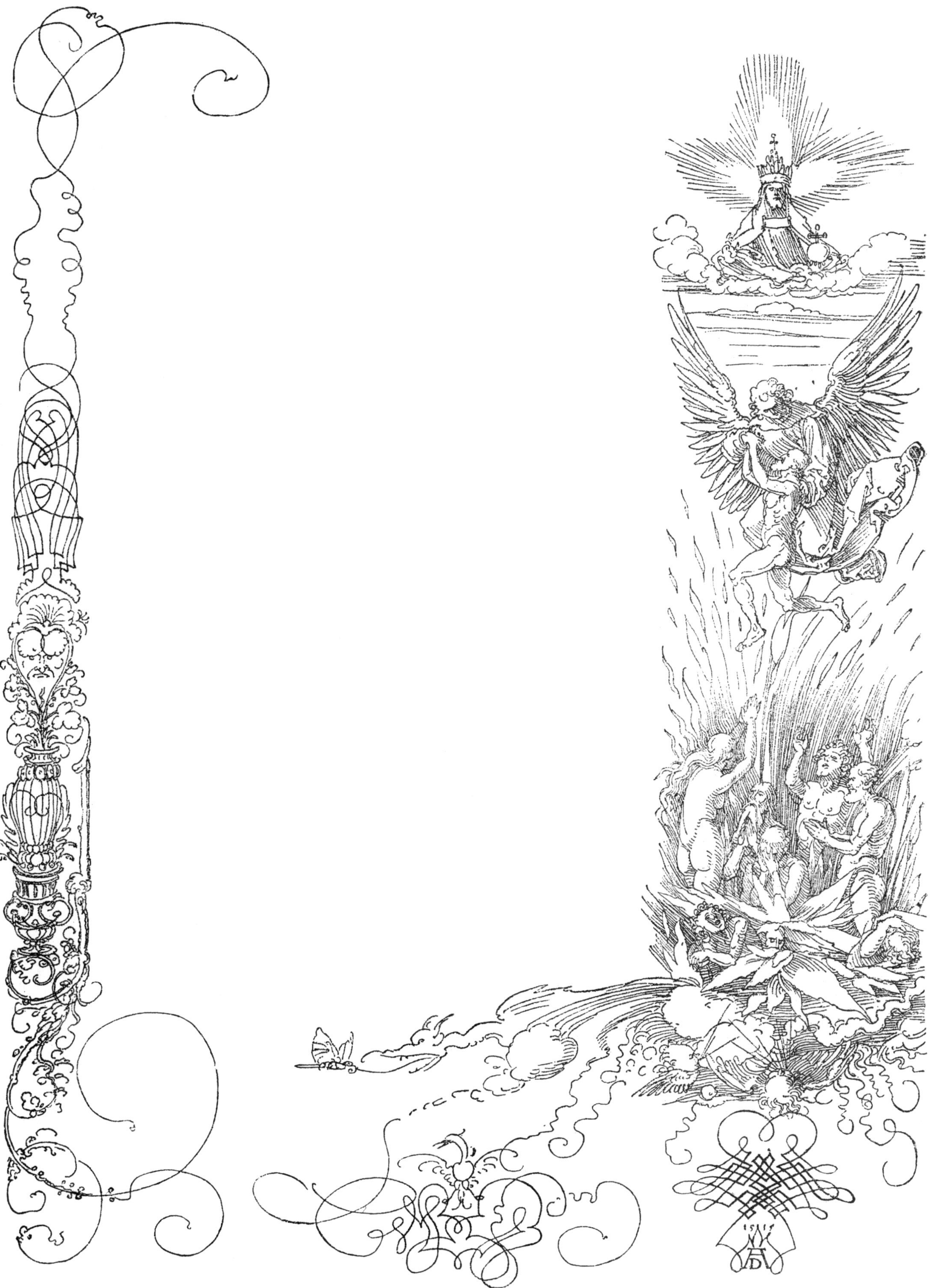

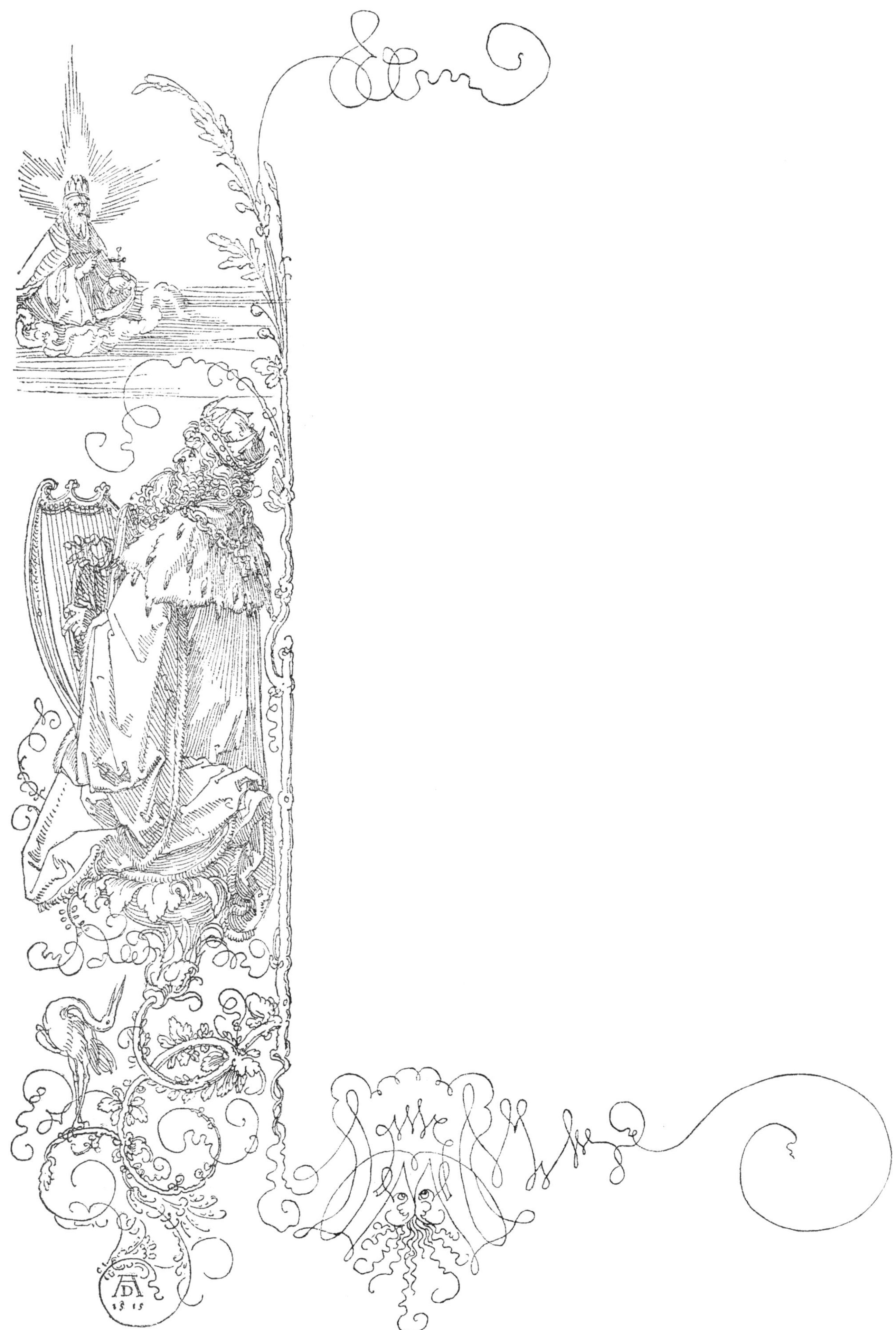

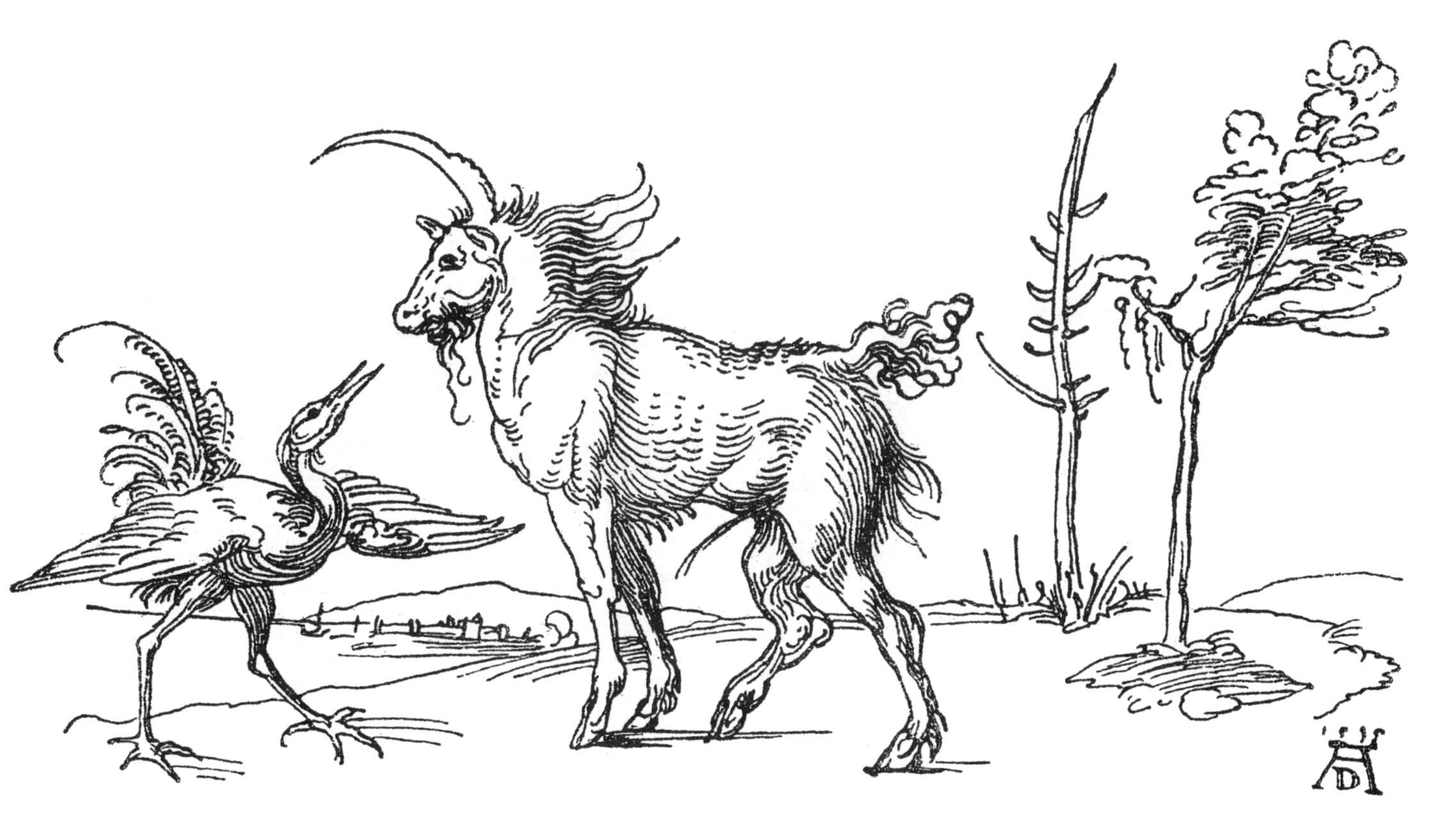

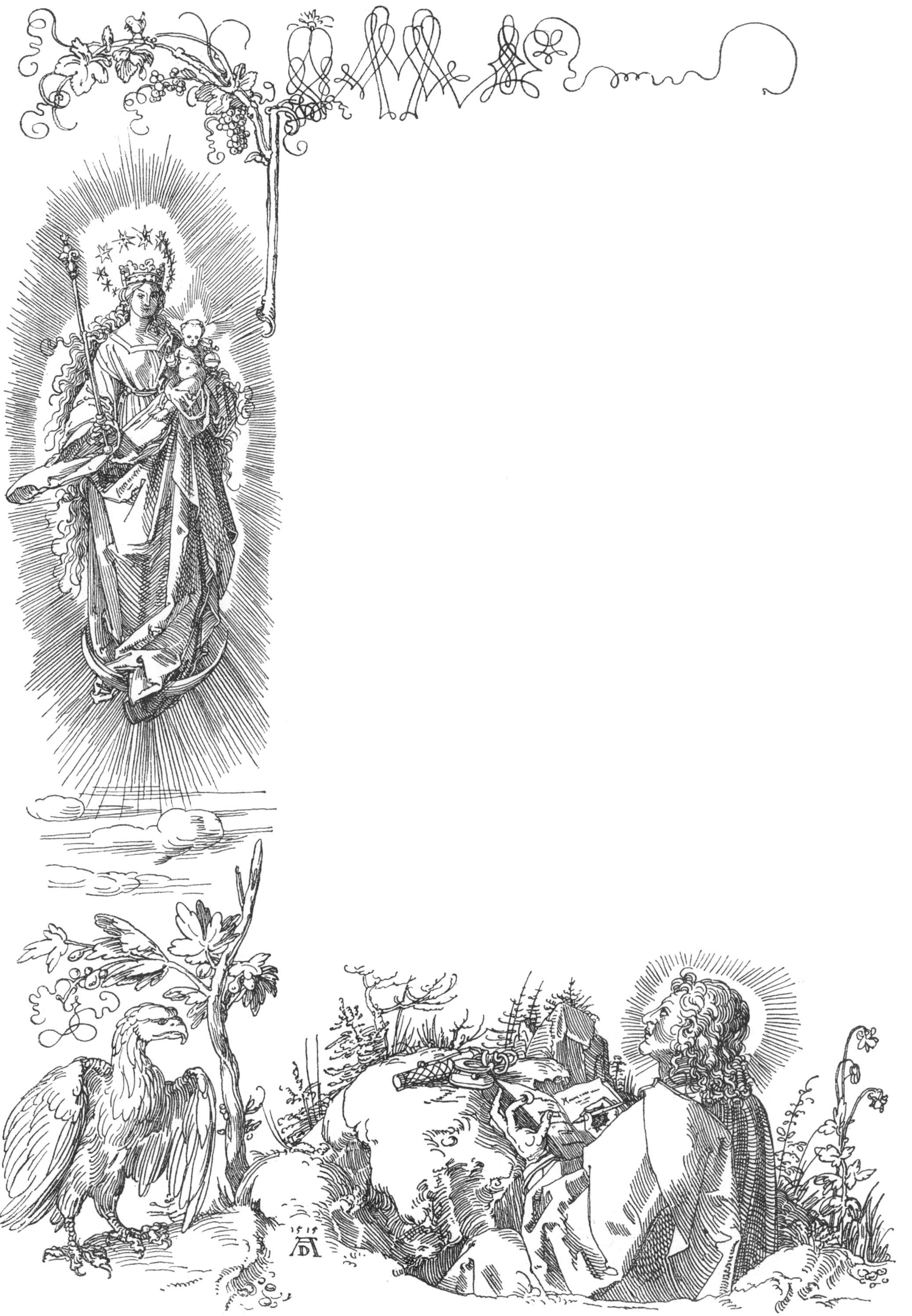

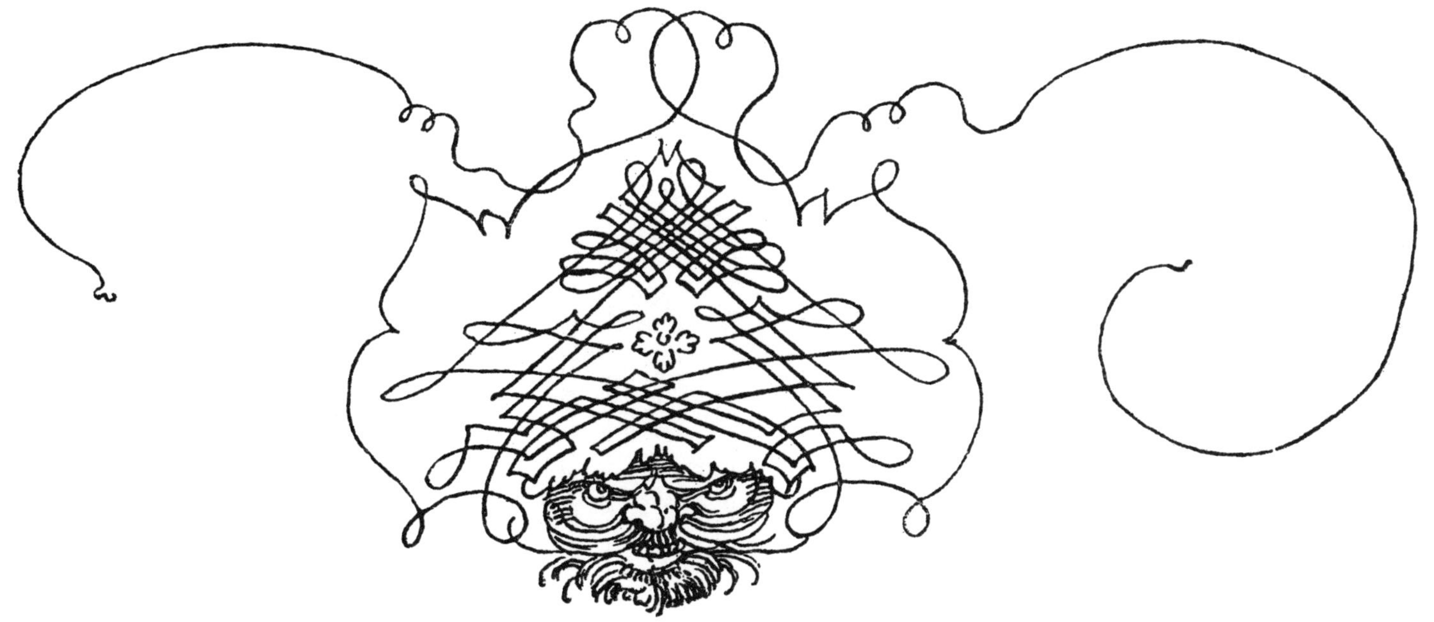

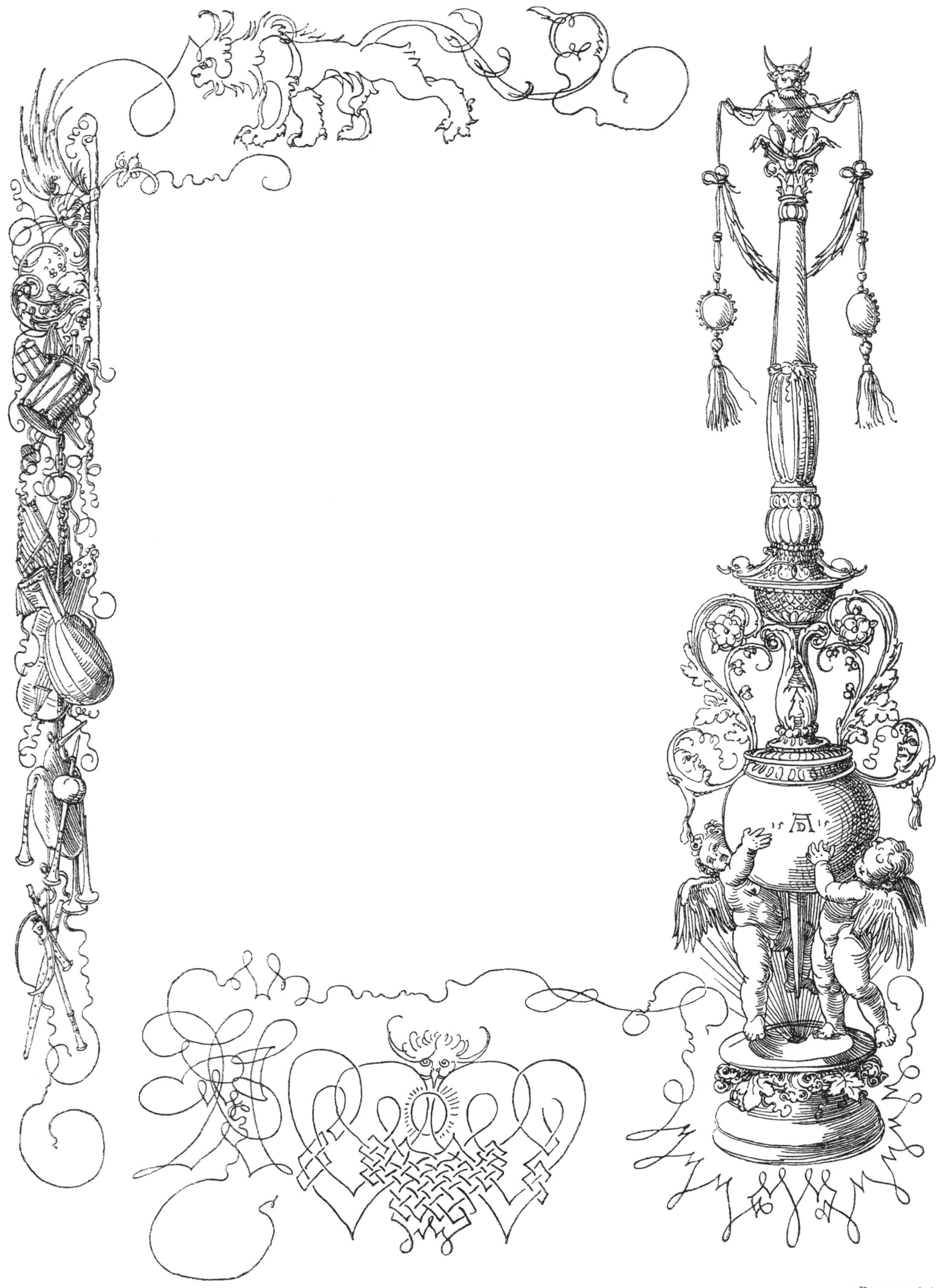

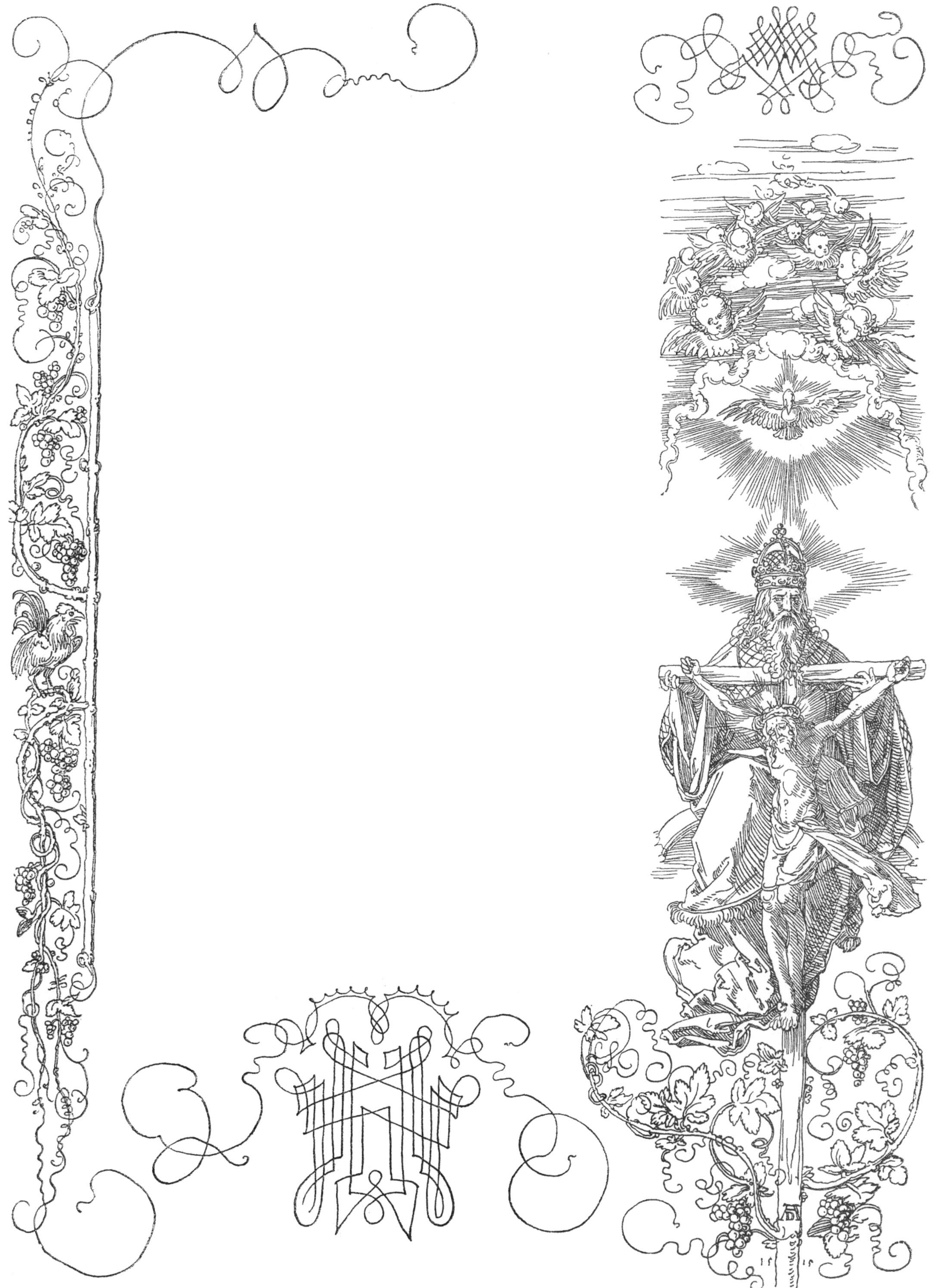

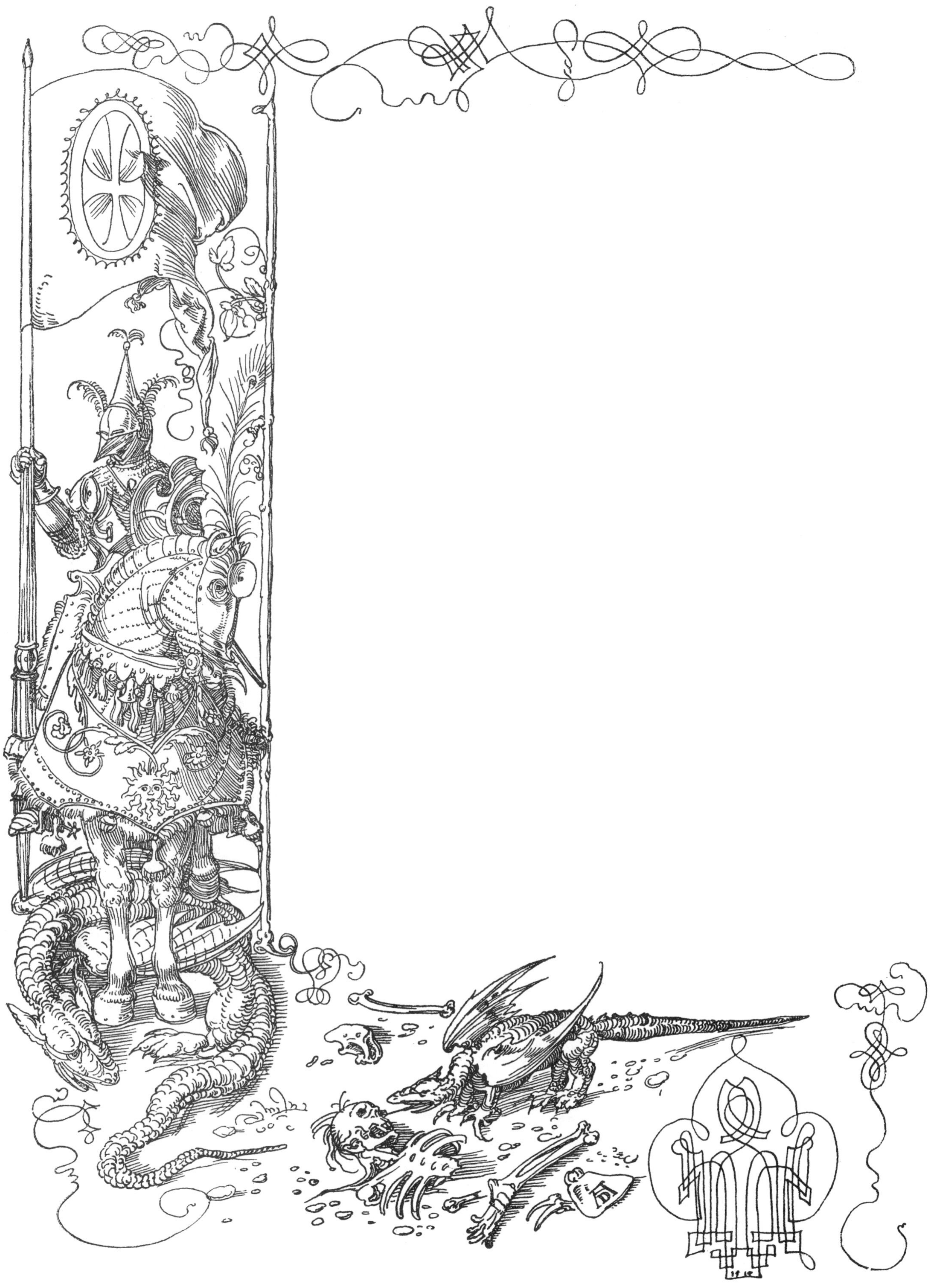

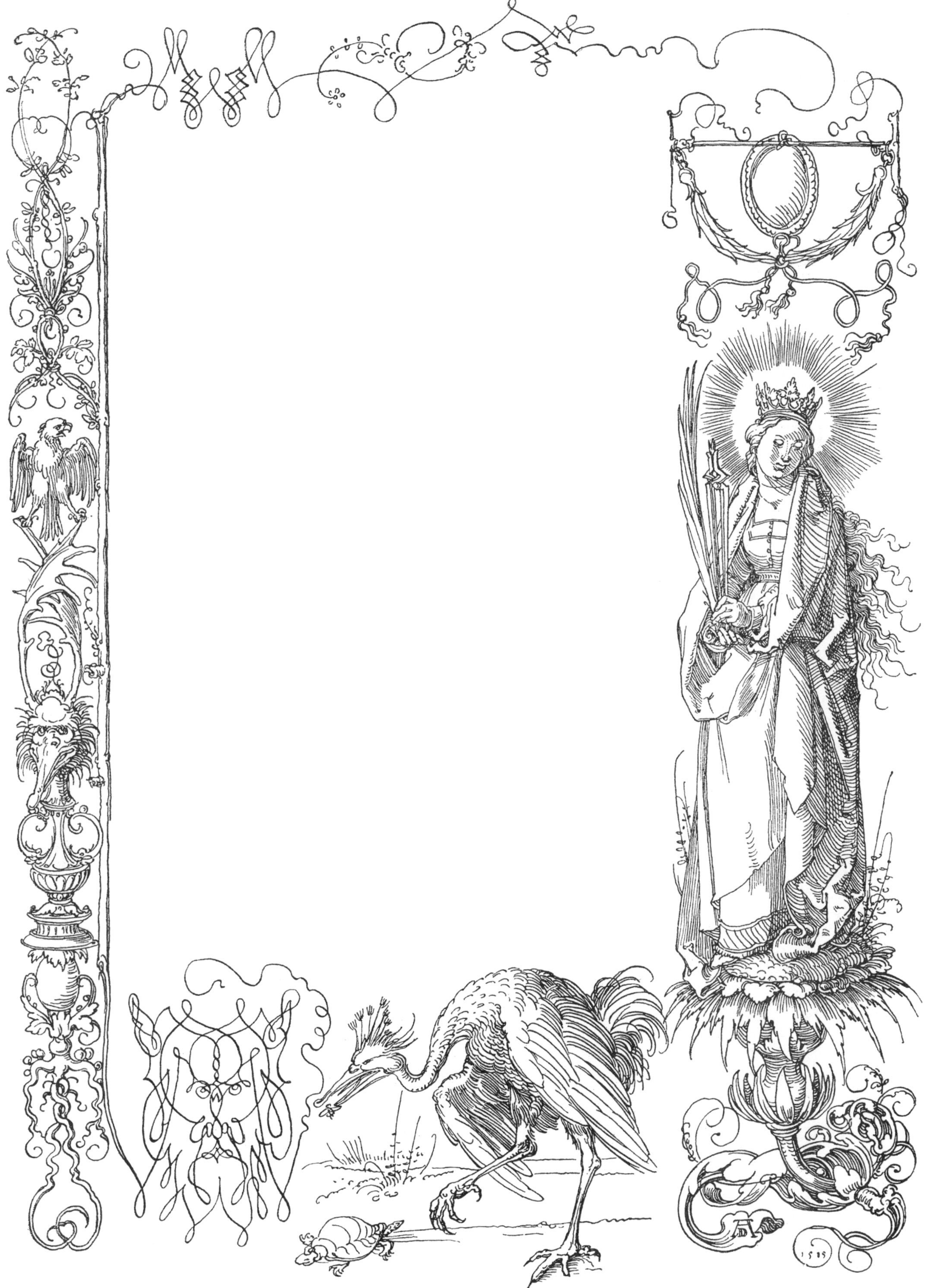

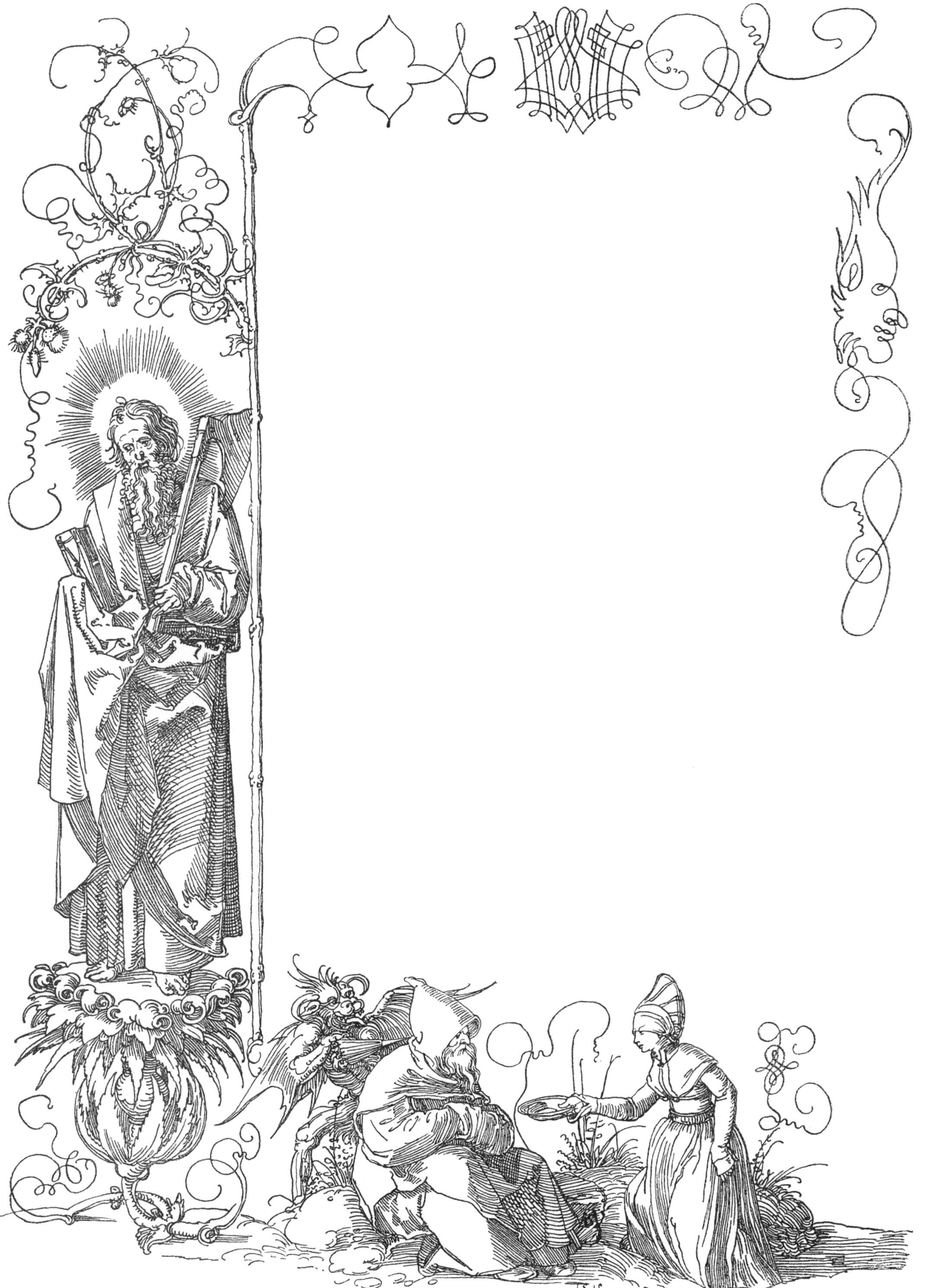

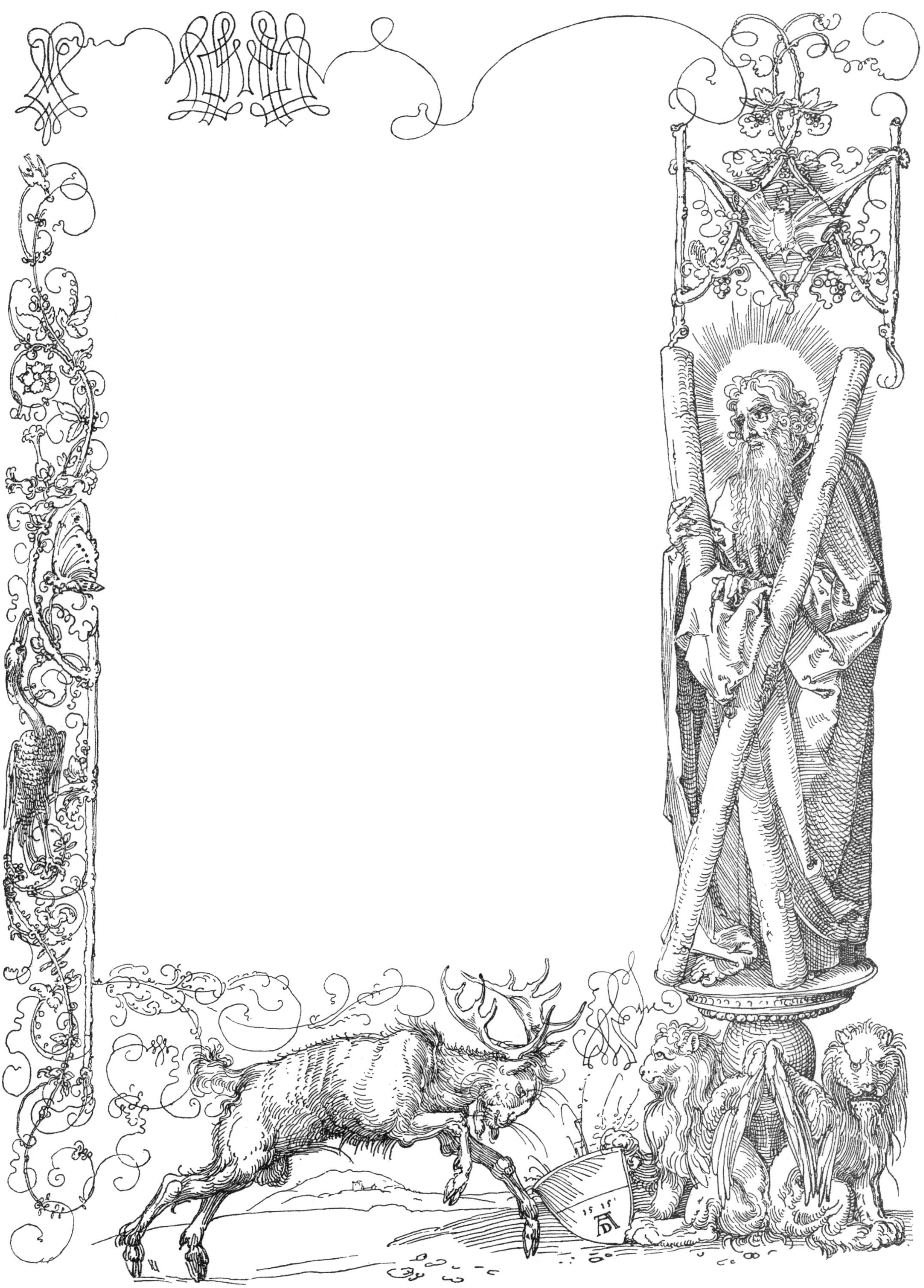

Plate 19

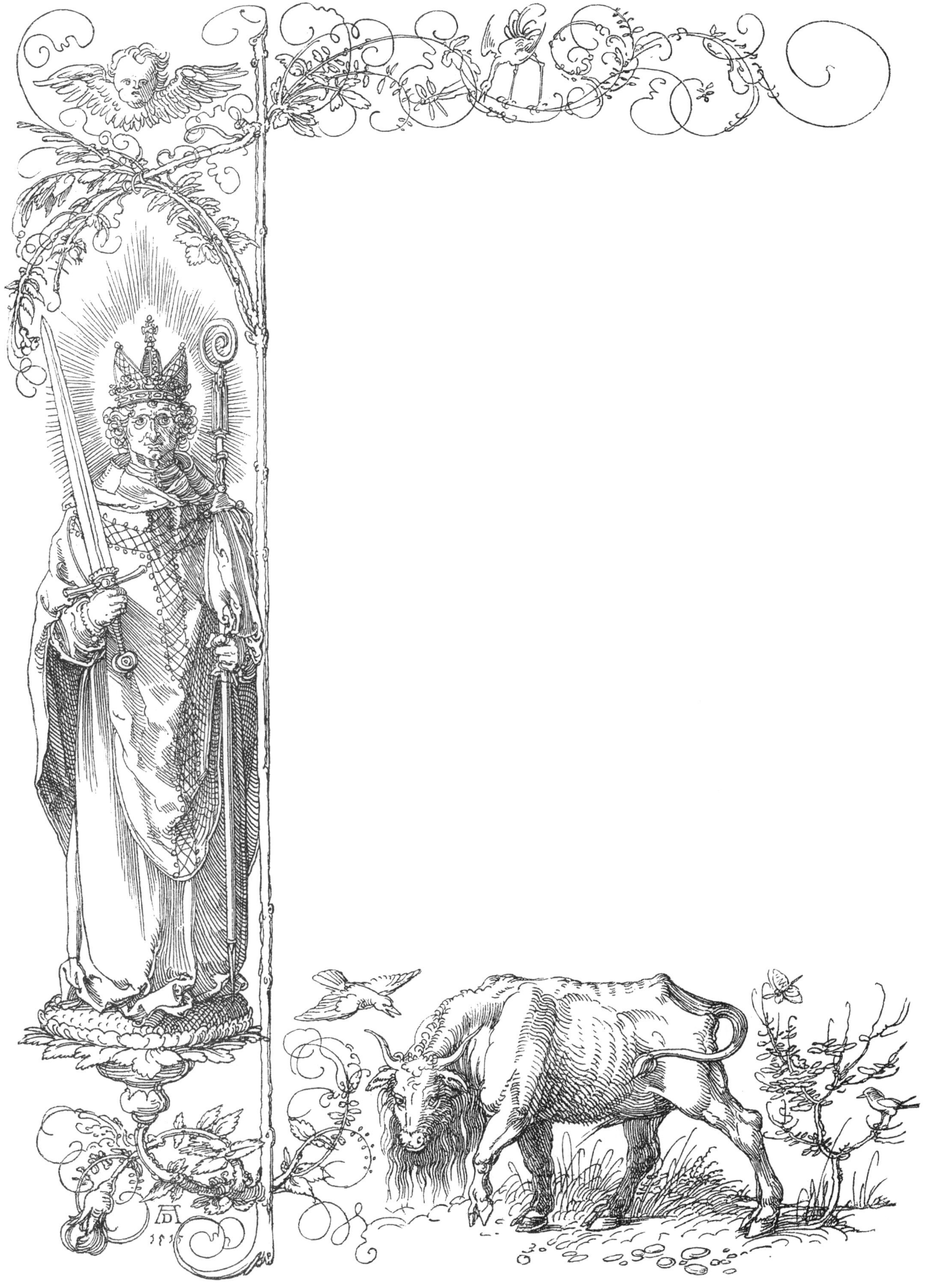

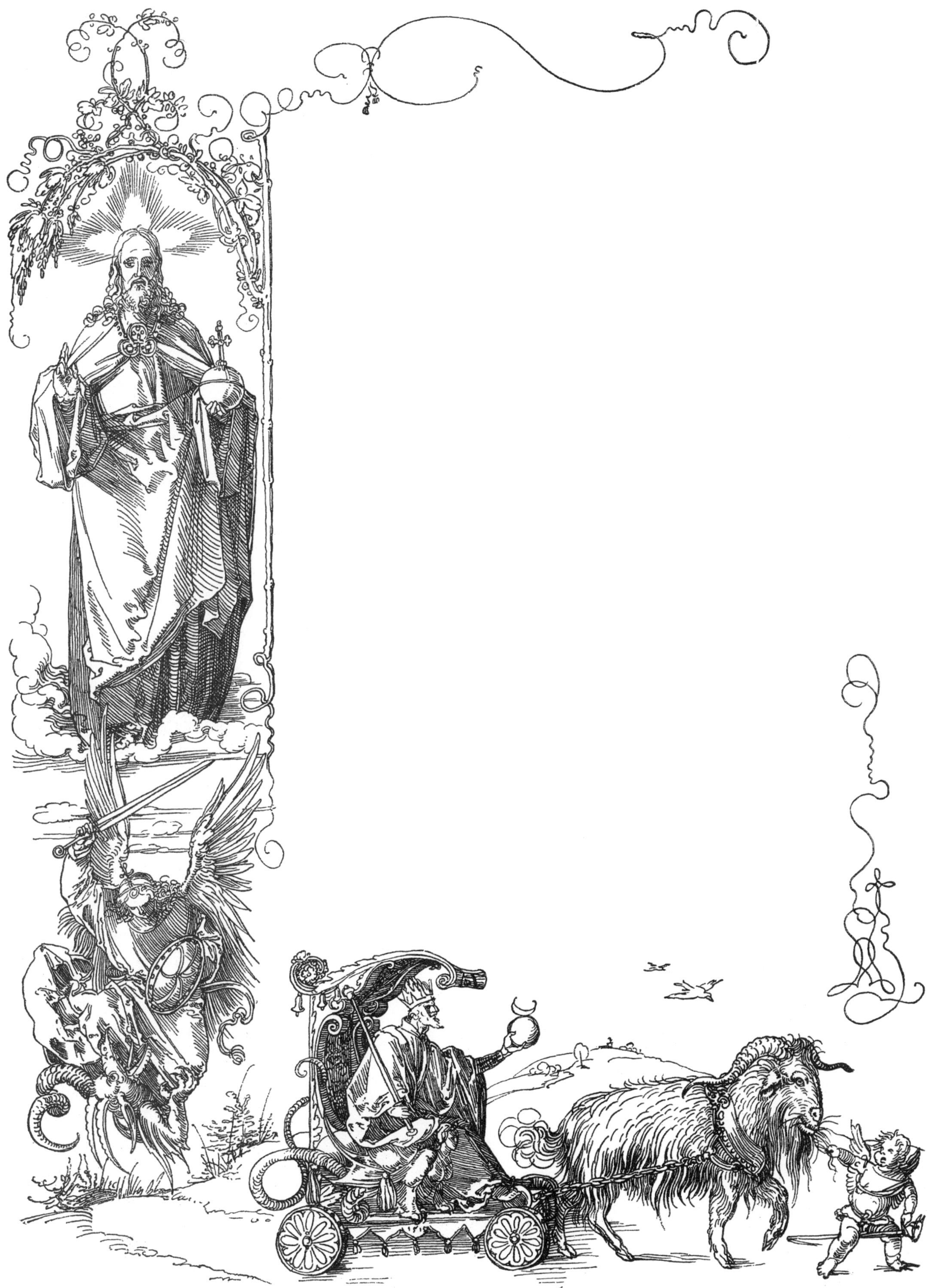

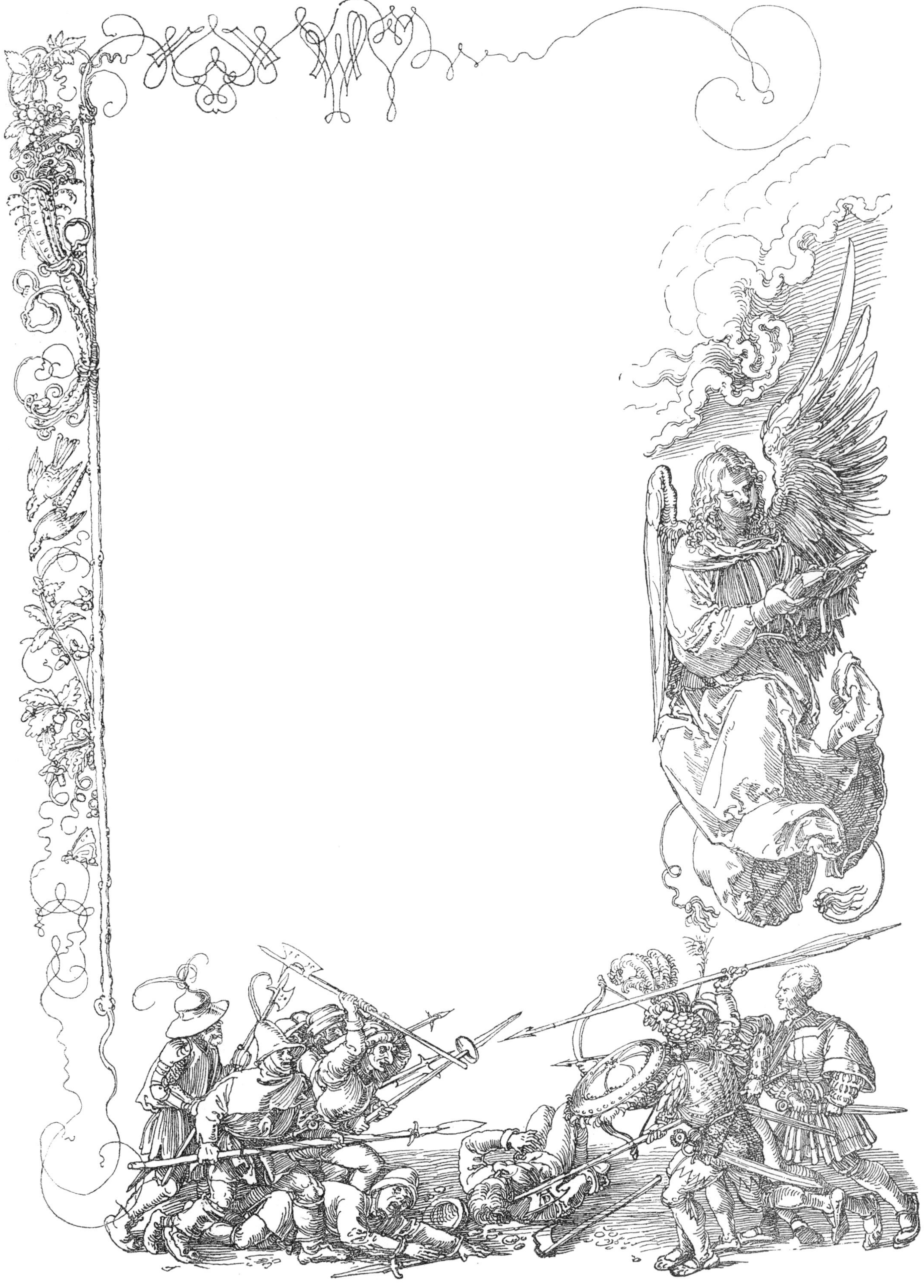

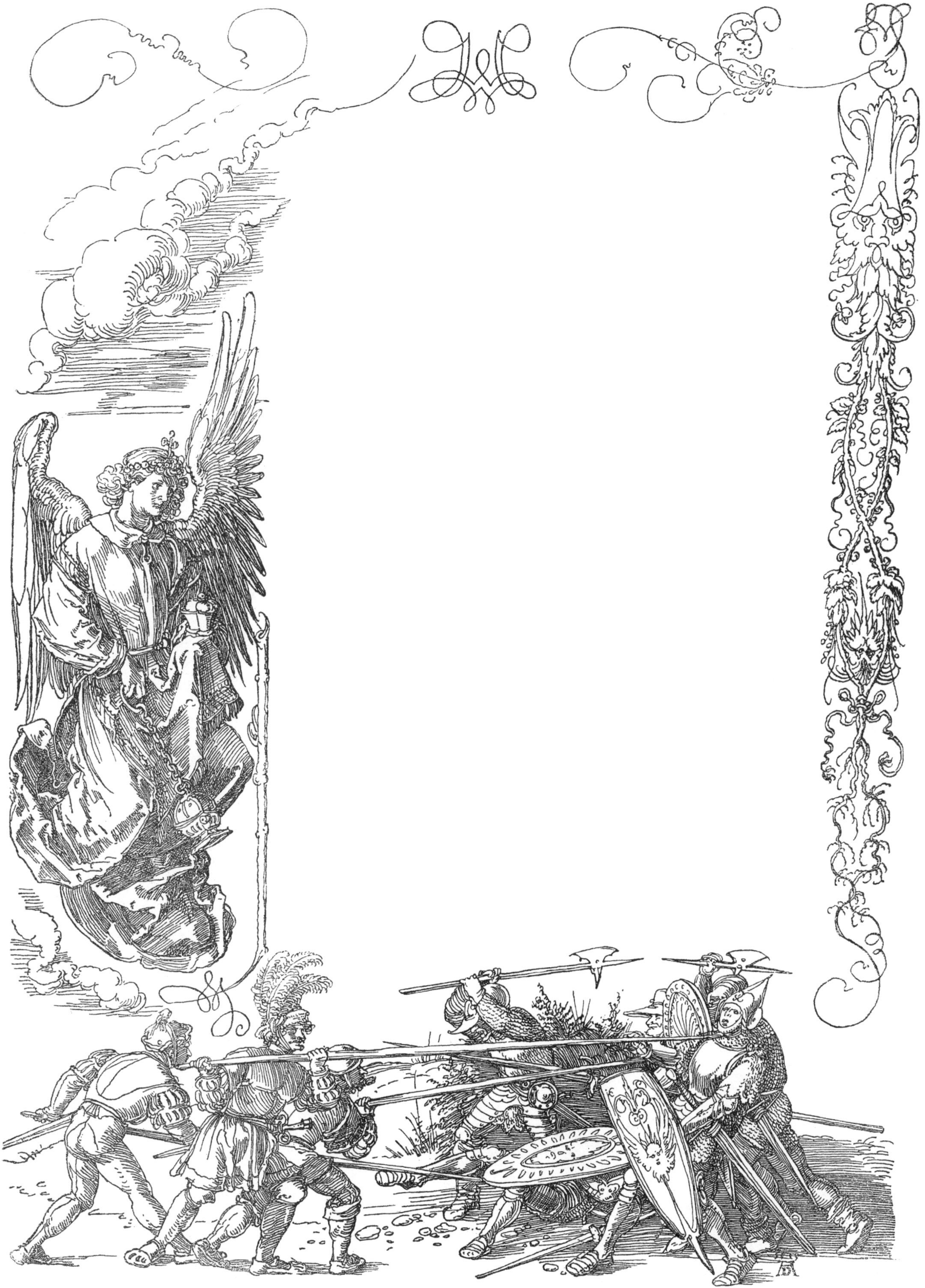

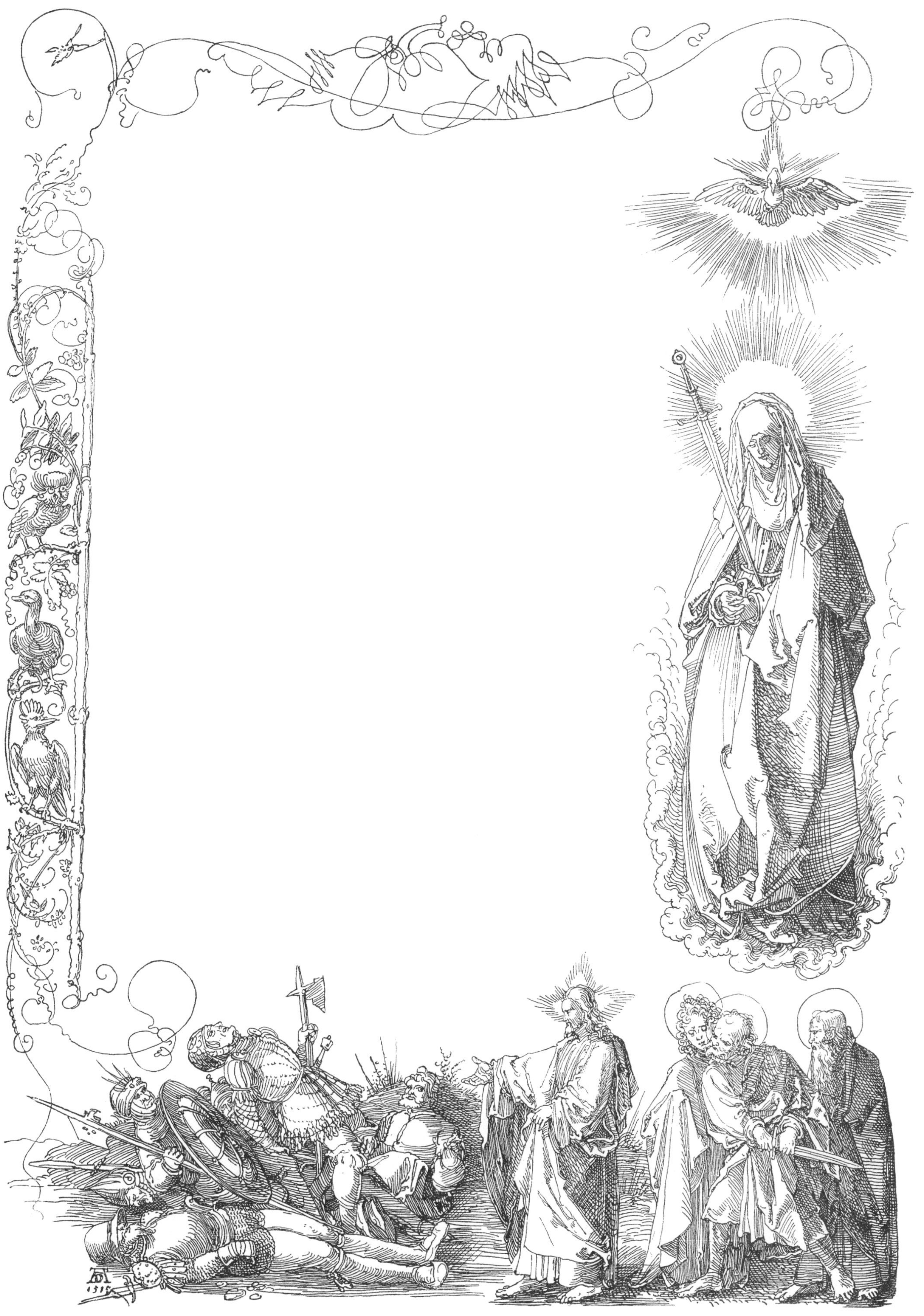

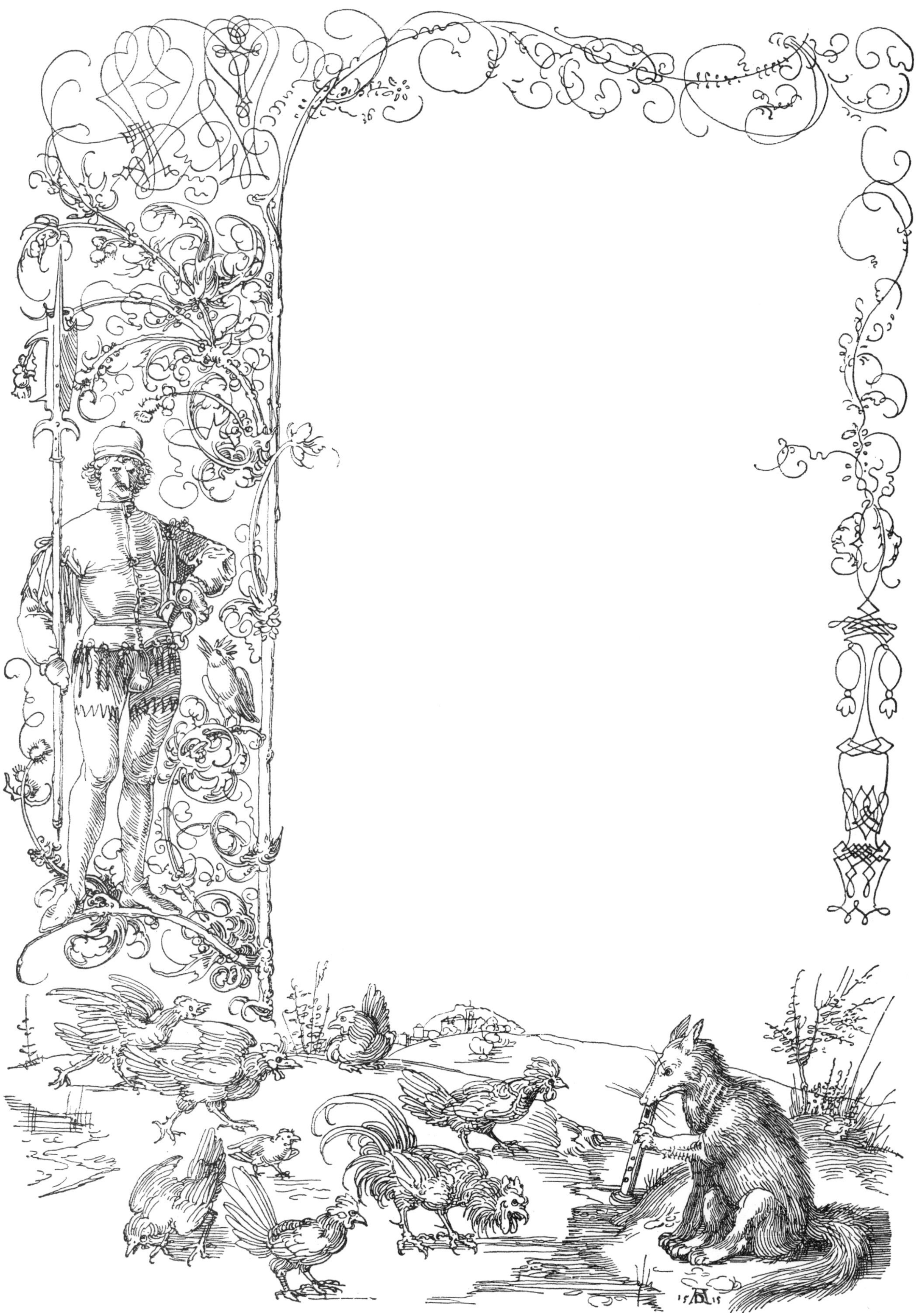

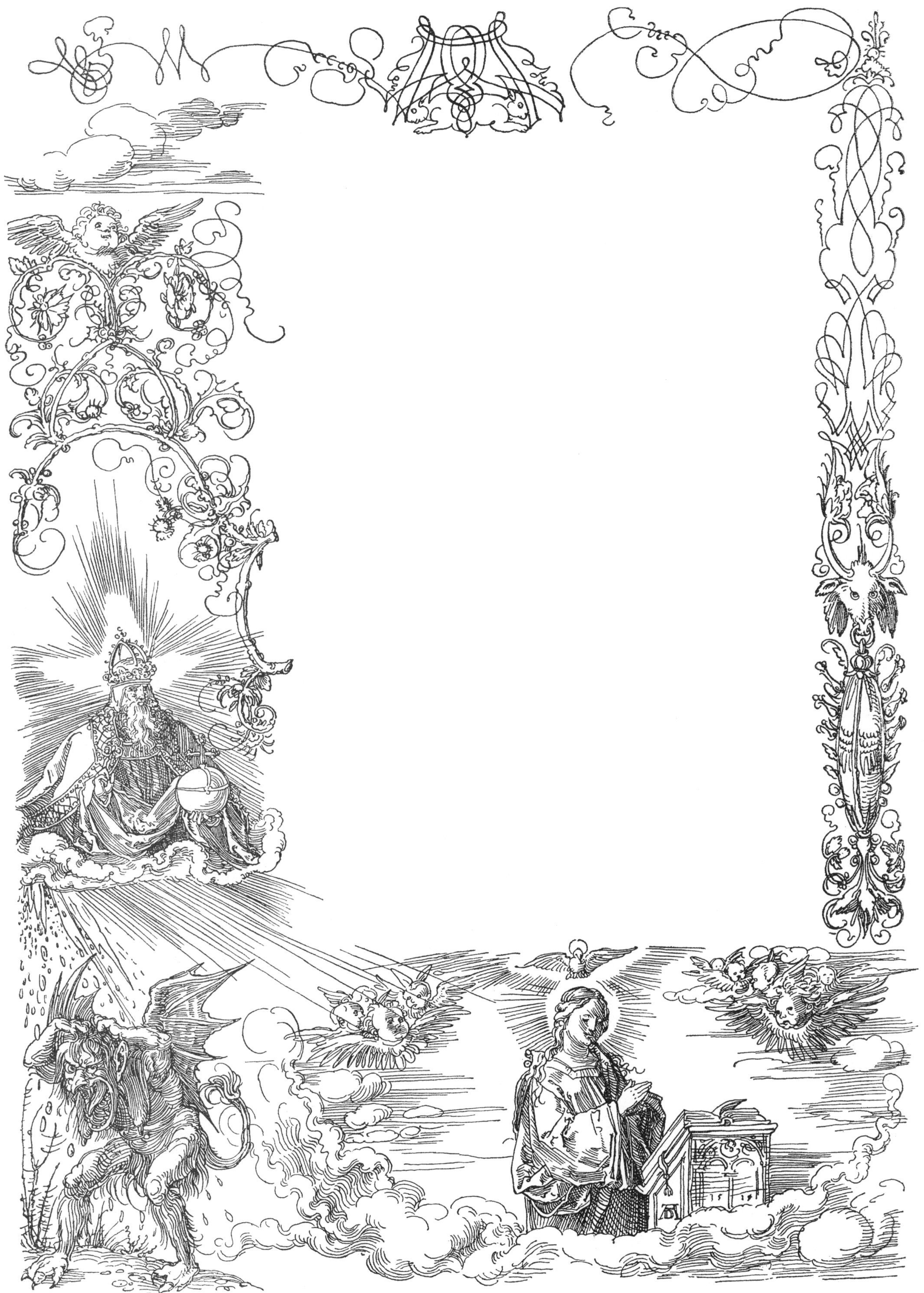

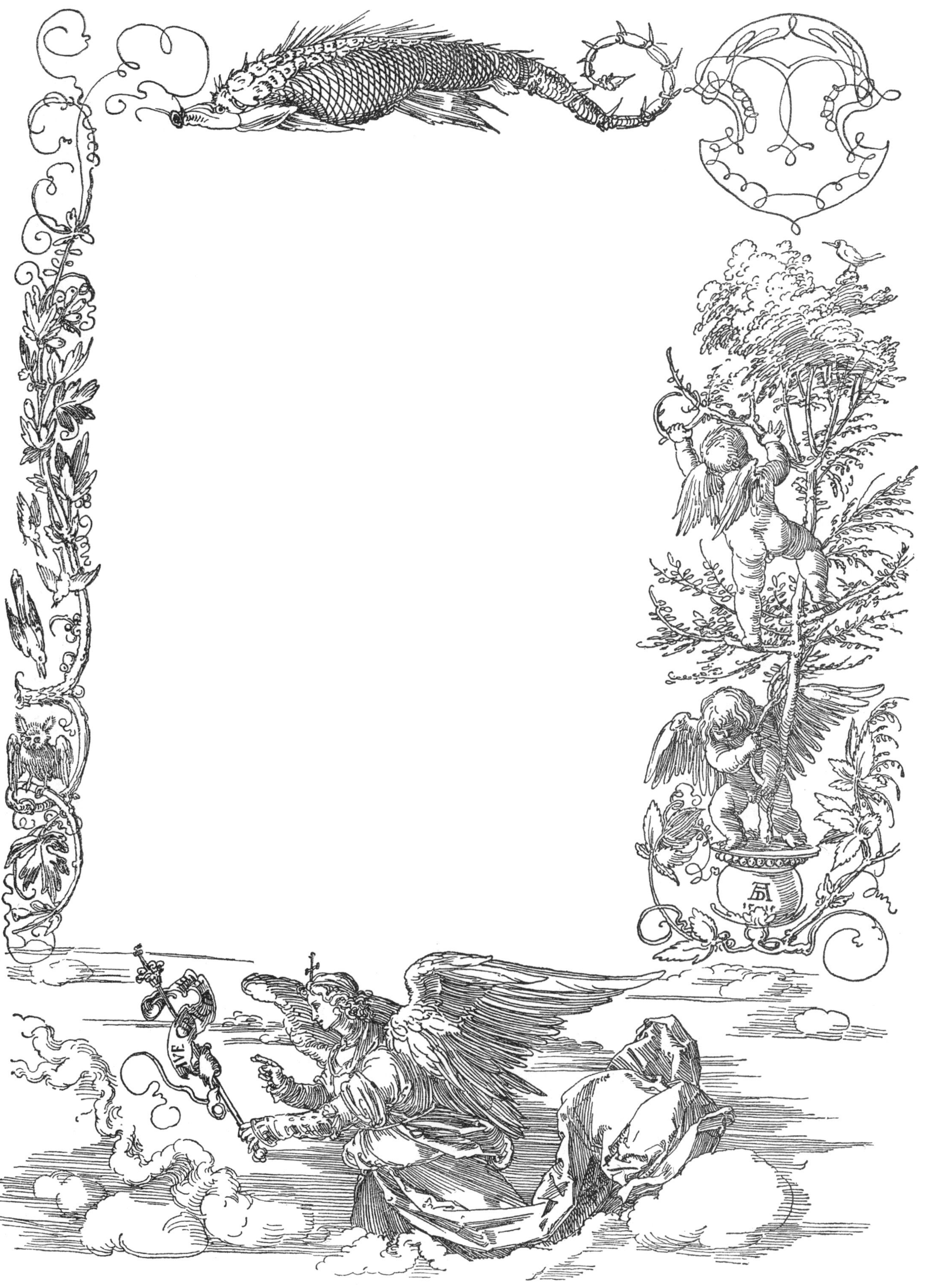

Plate 27

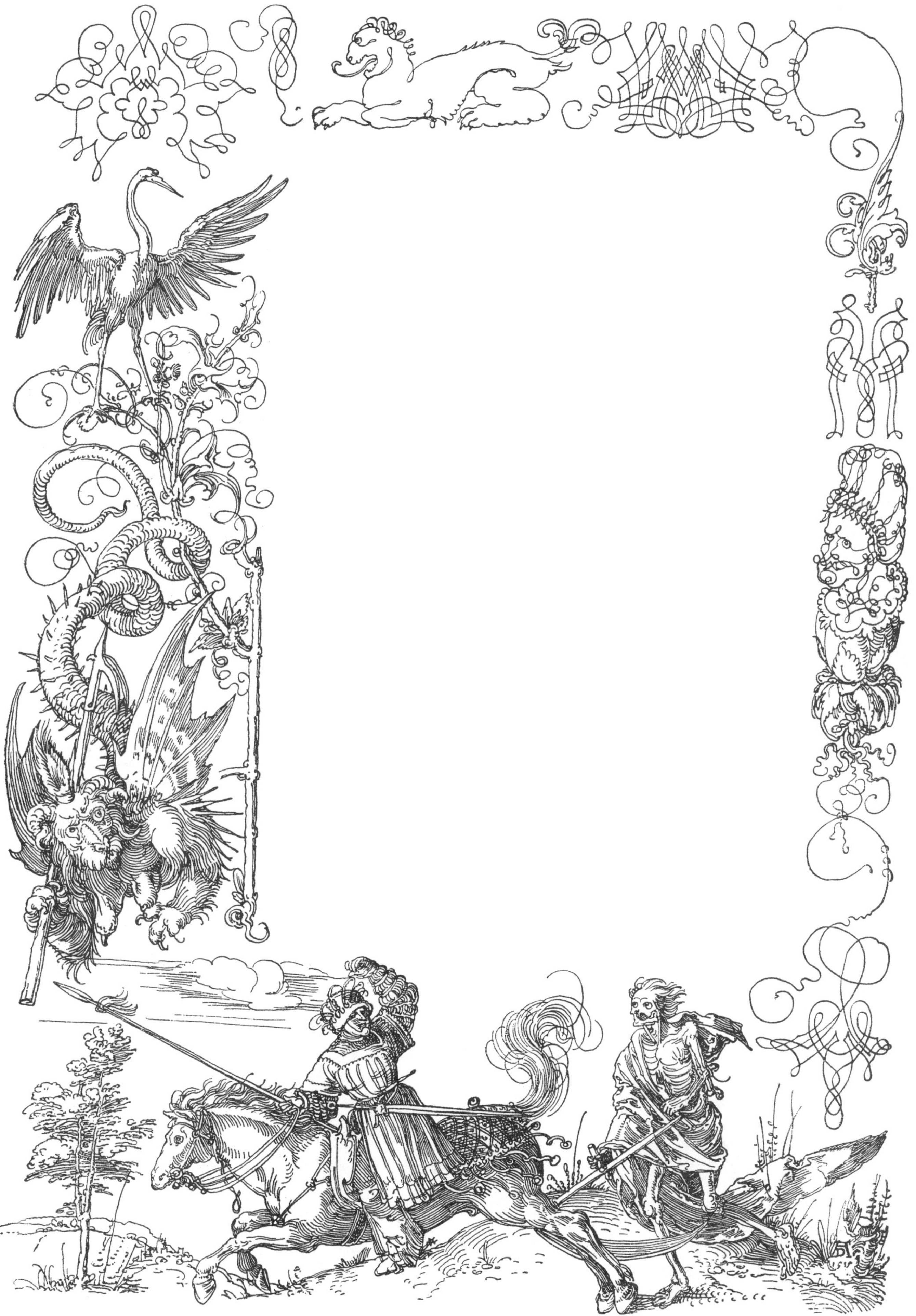

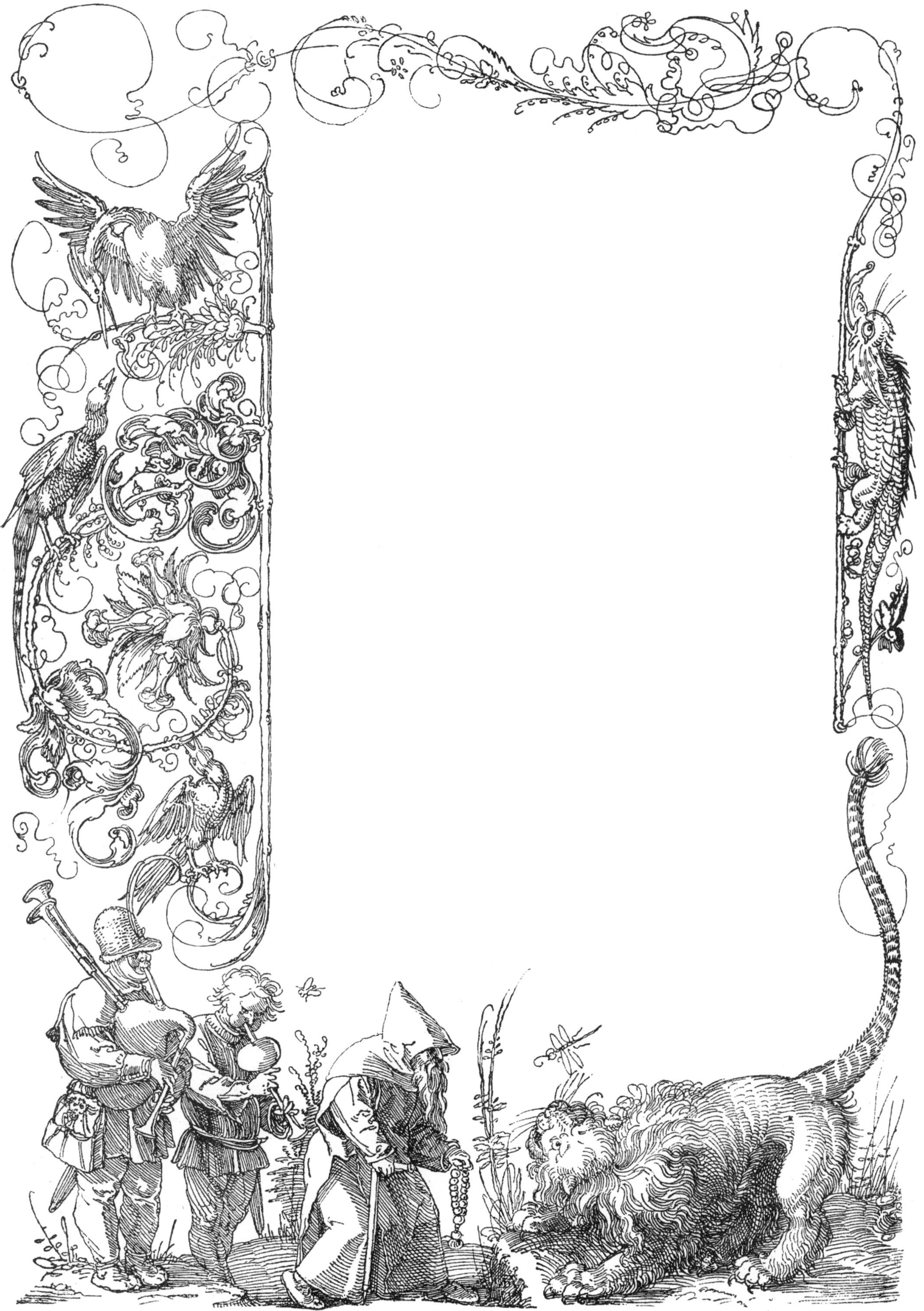

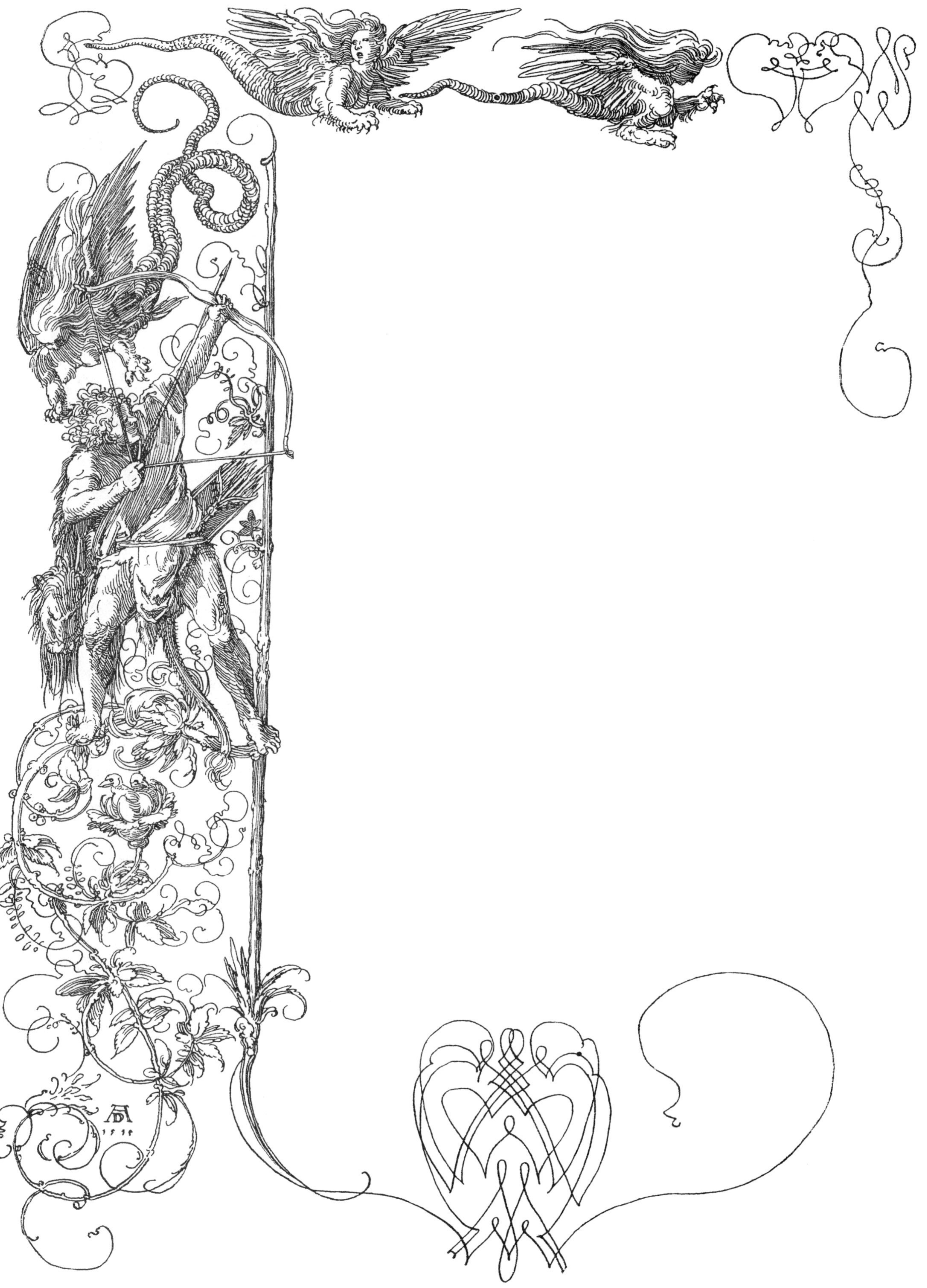

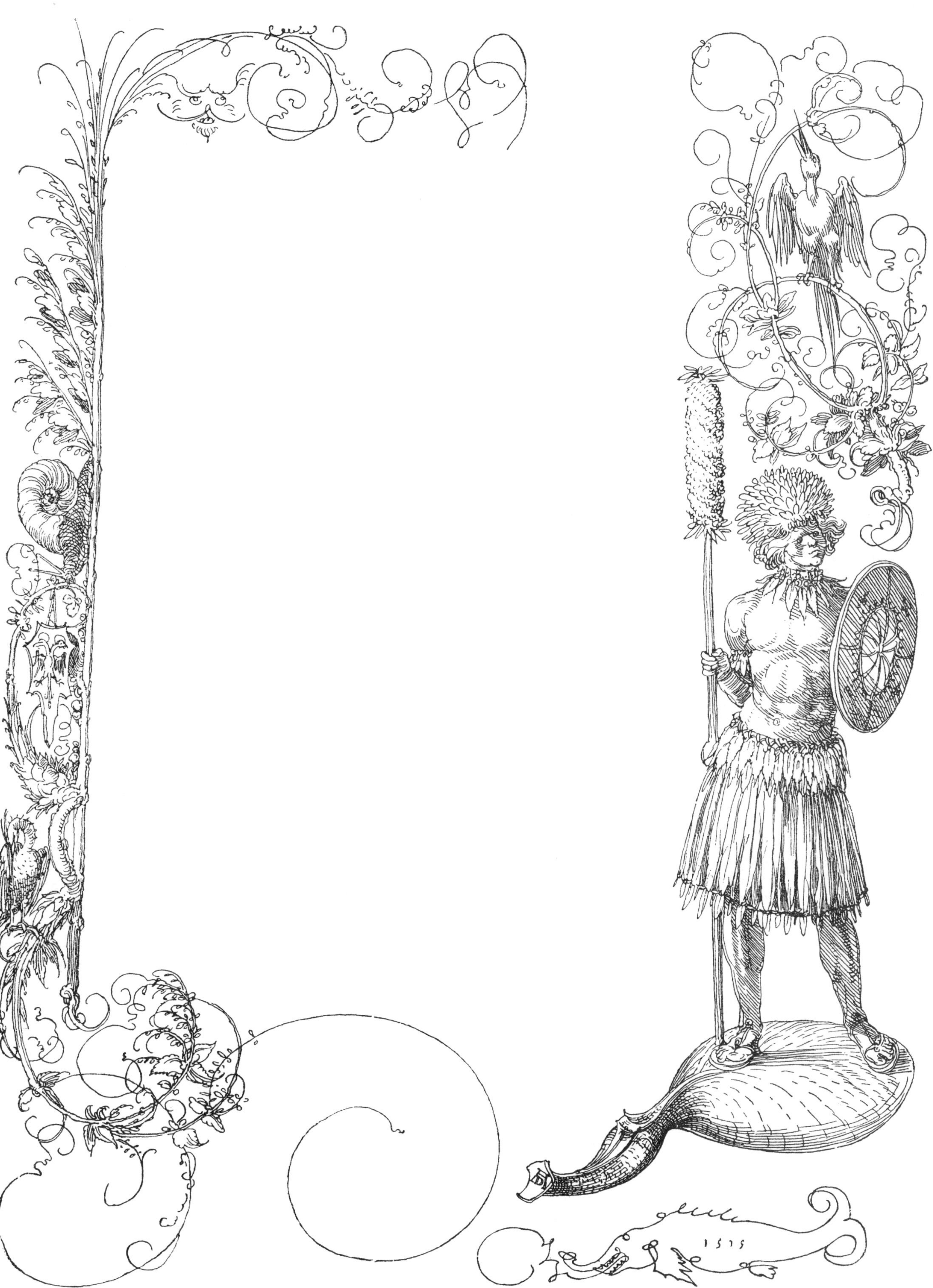

PLATE 31

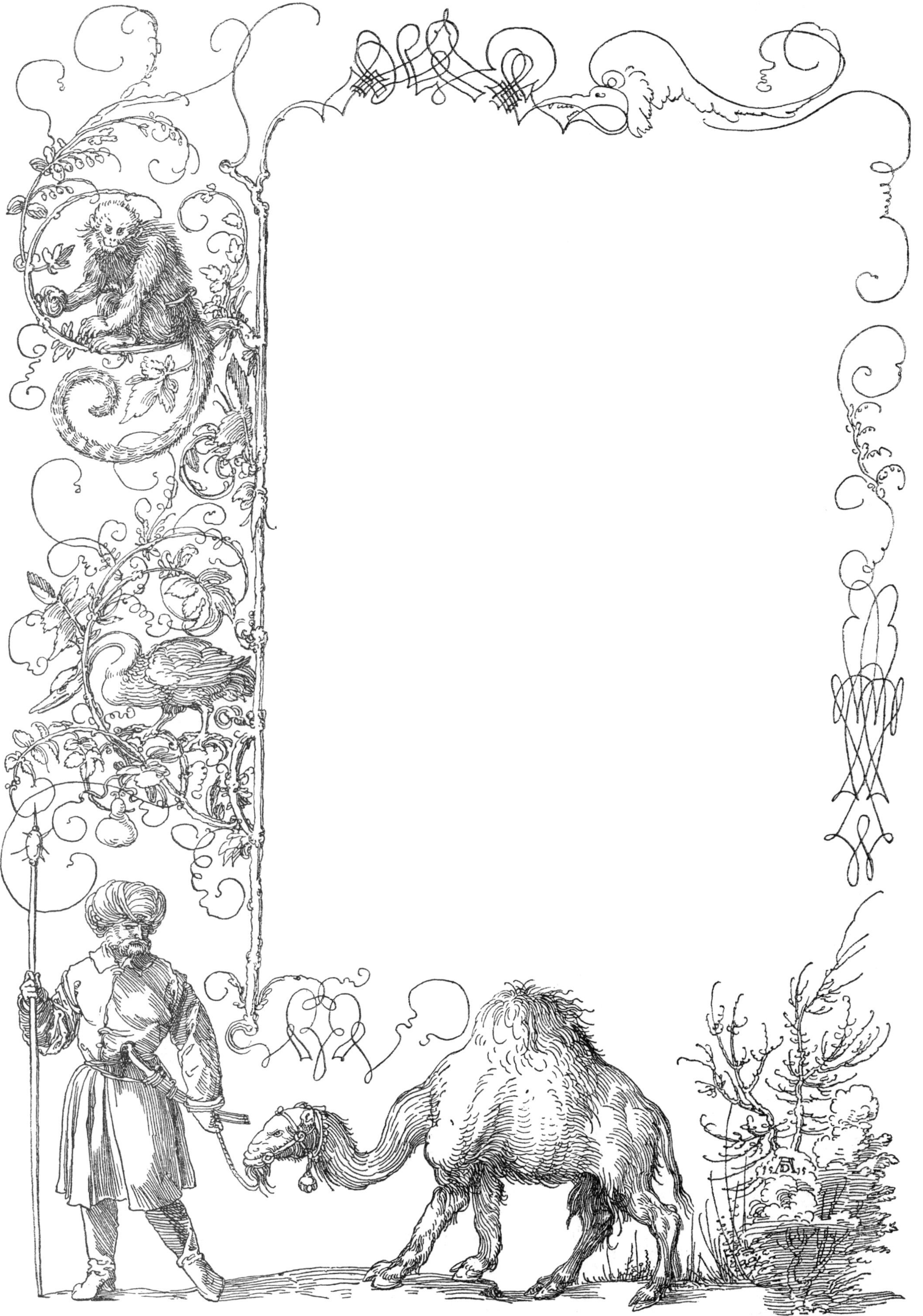

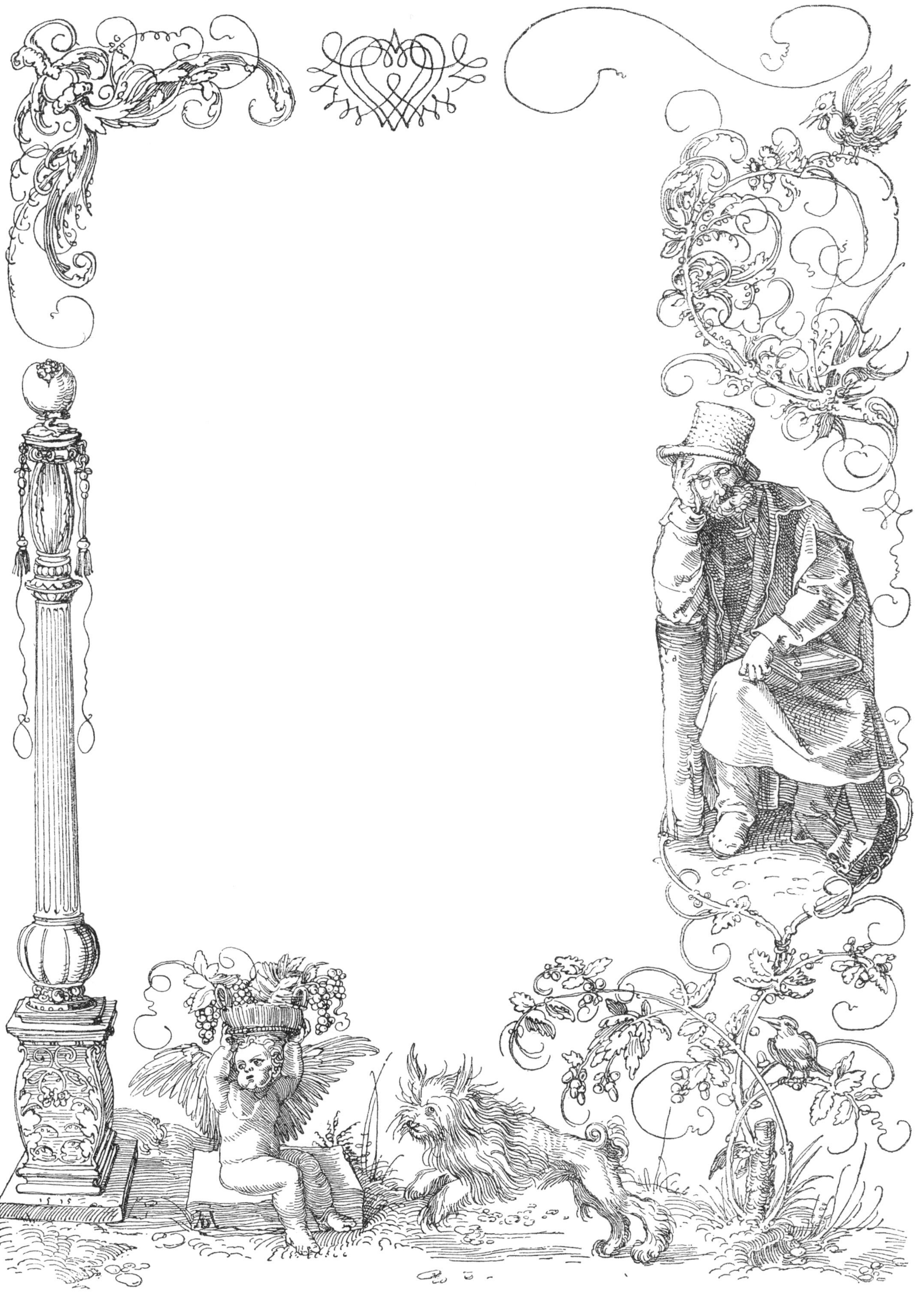

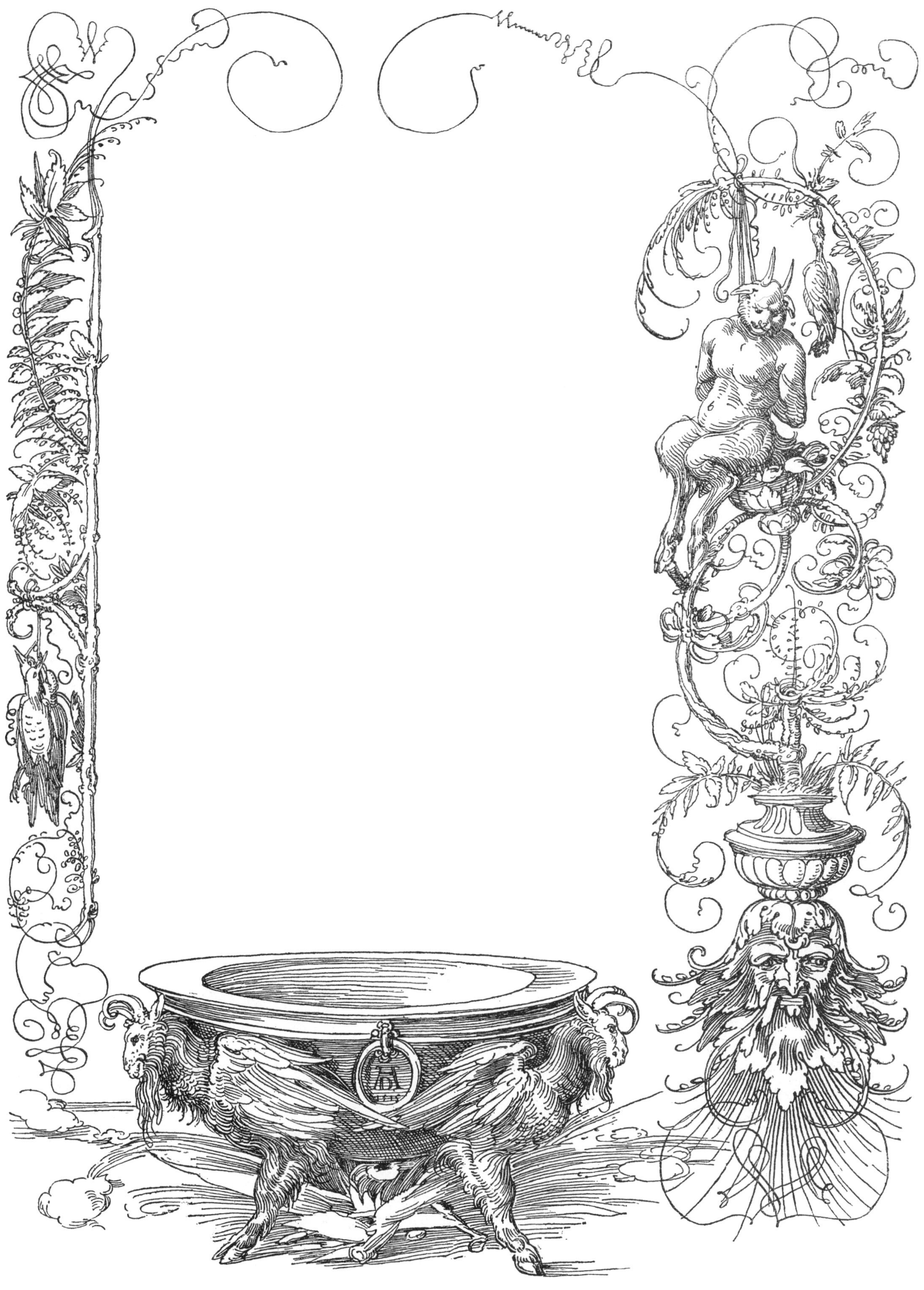

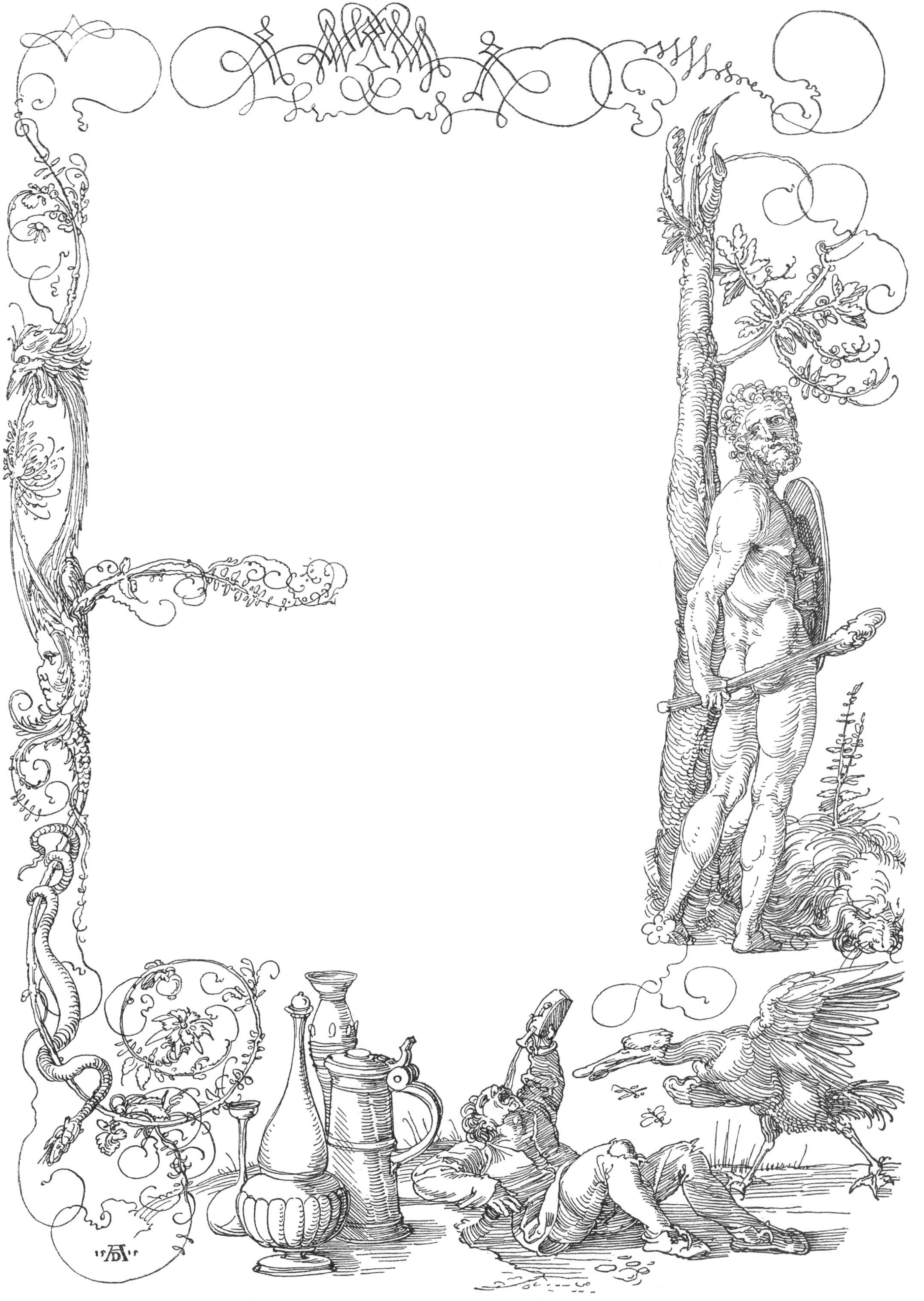

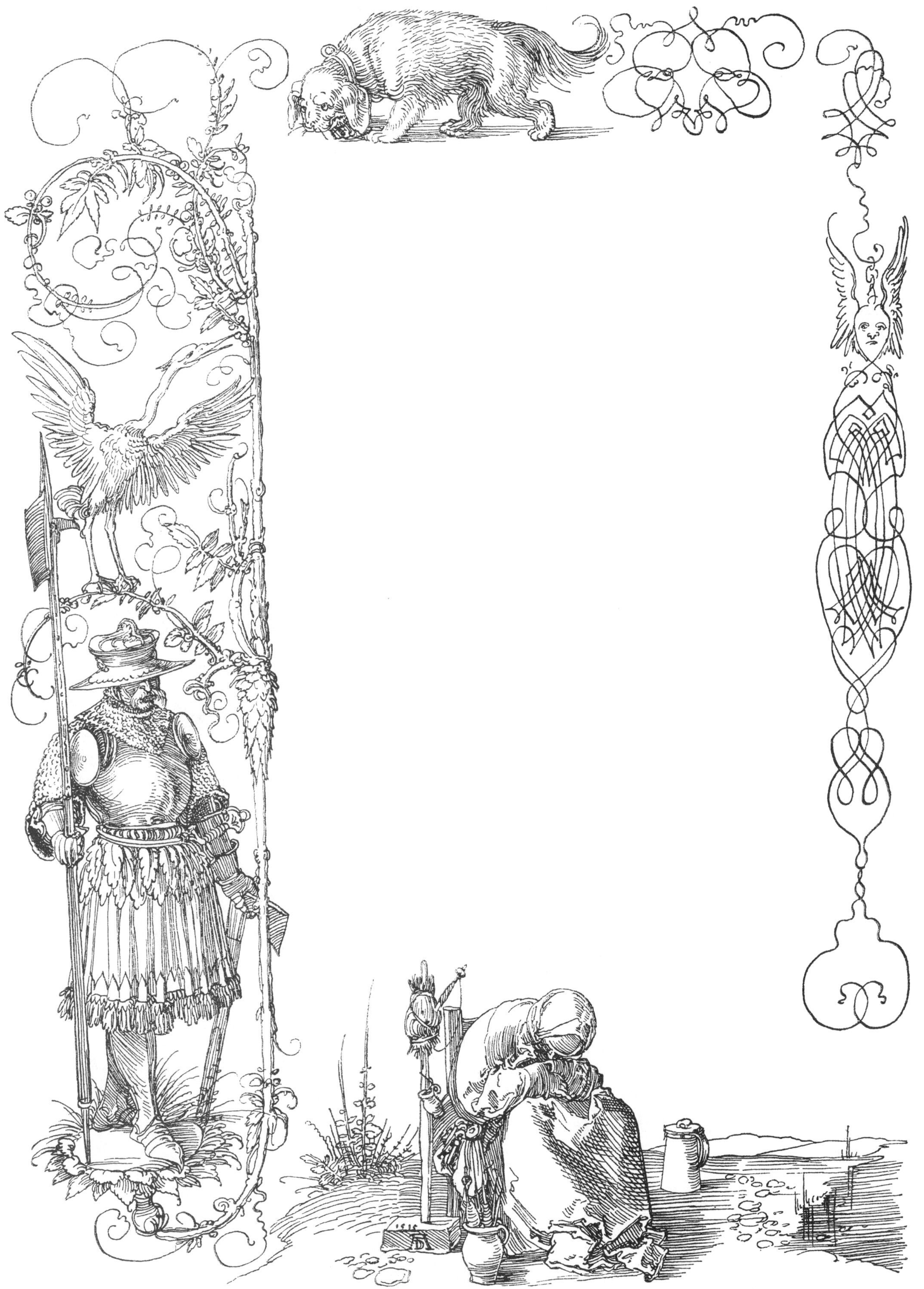

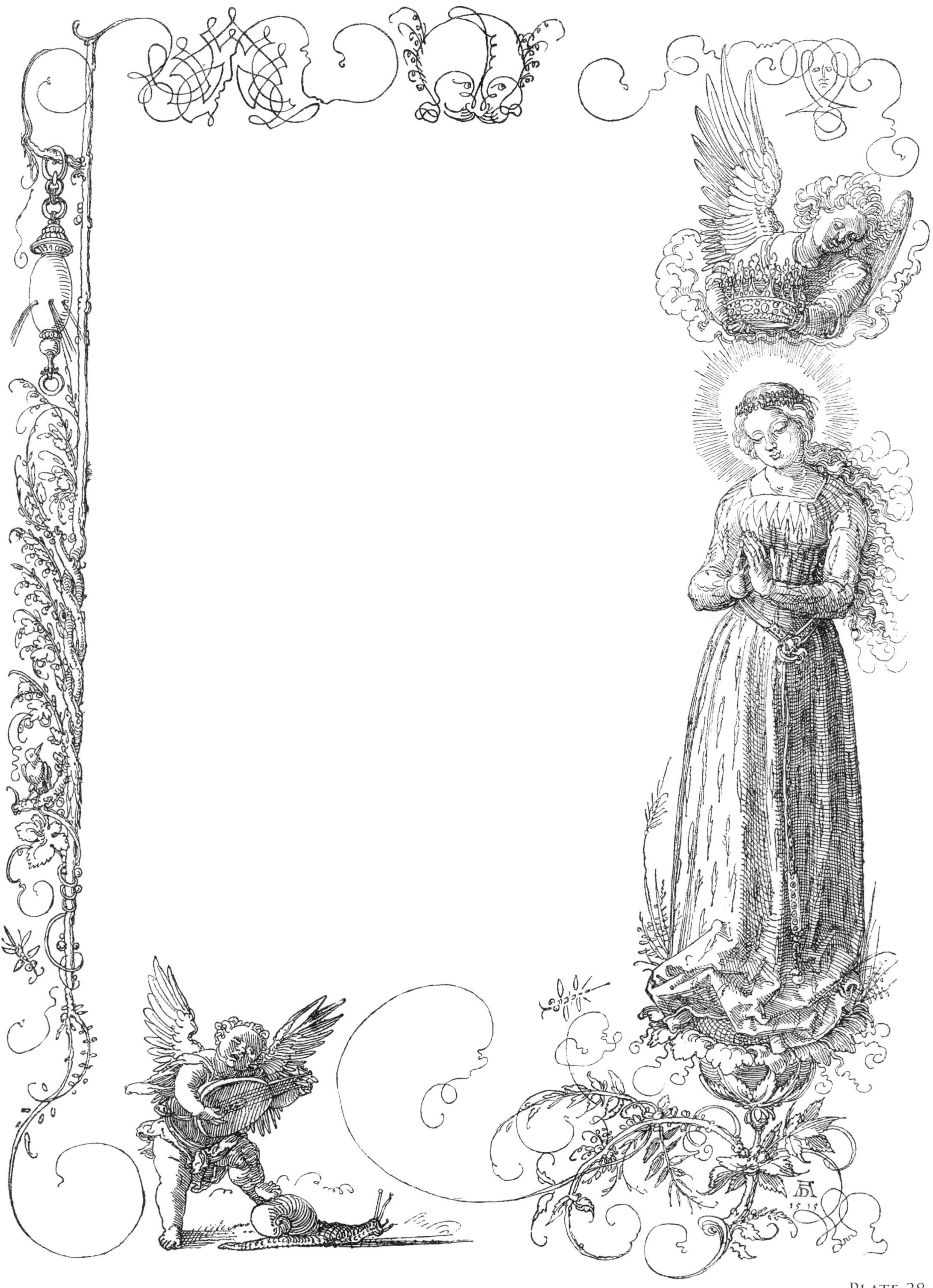

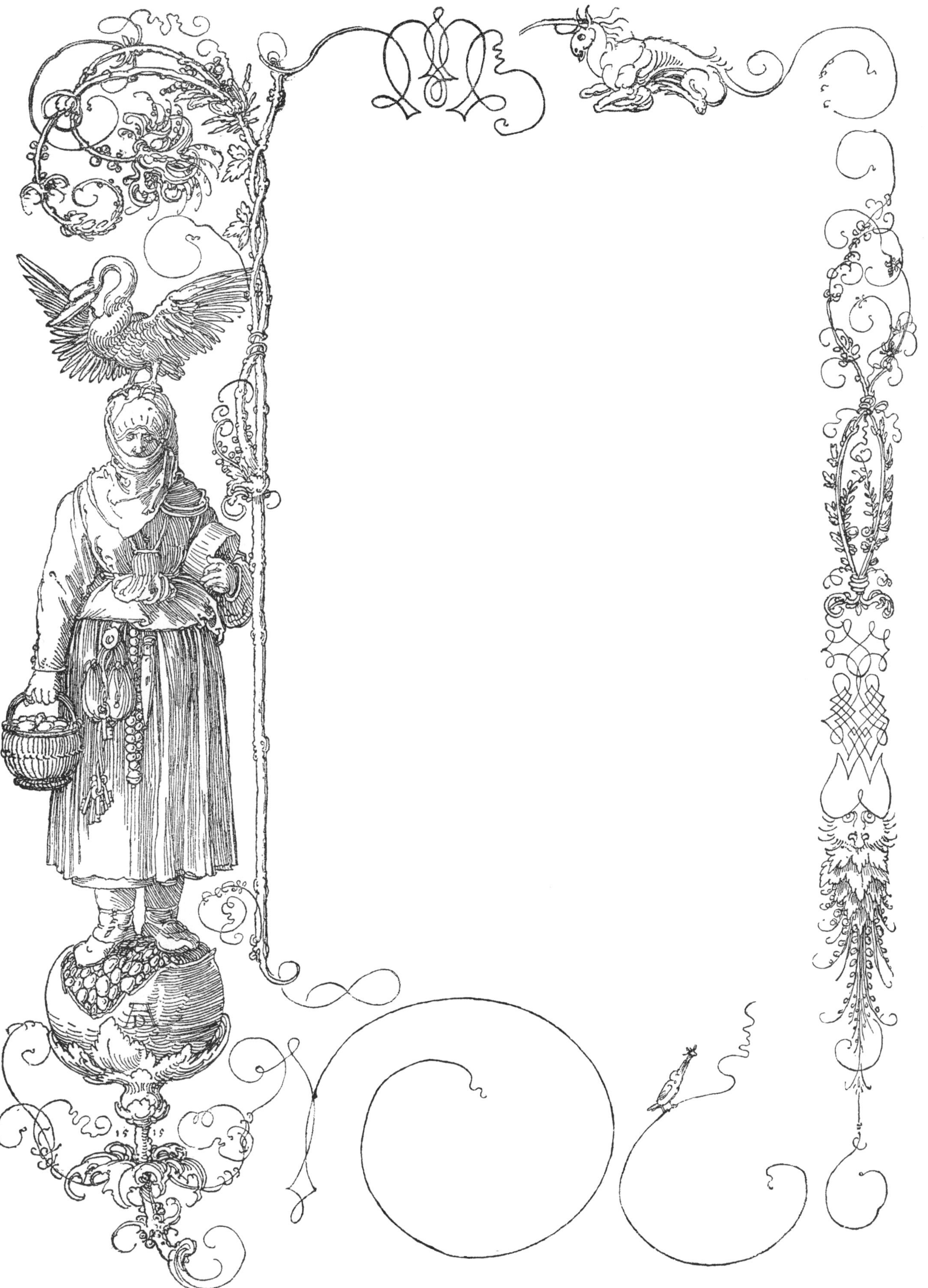

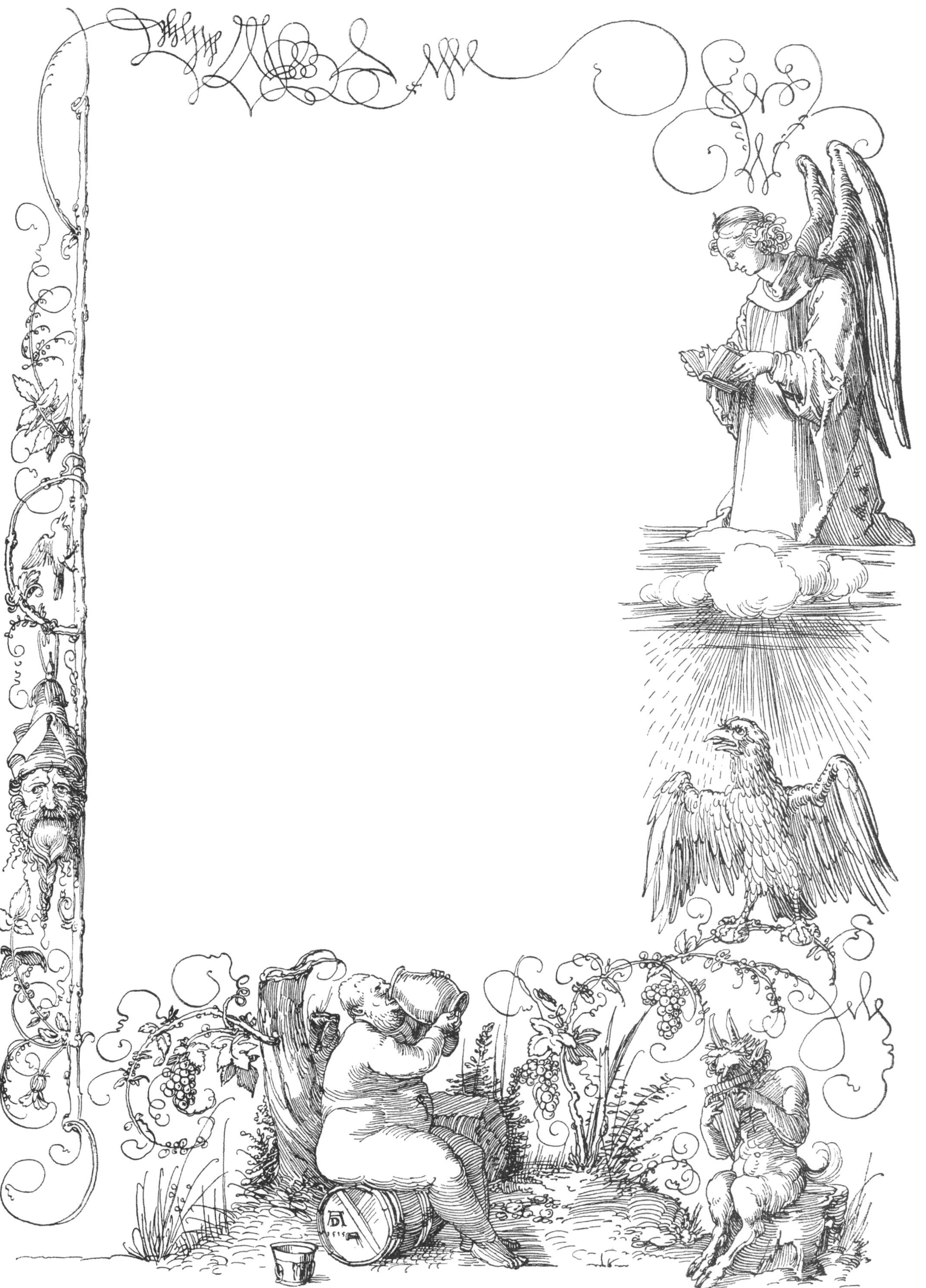

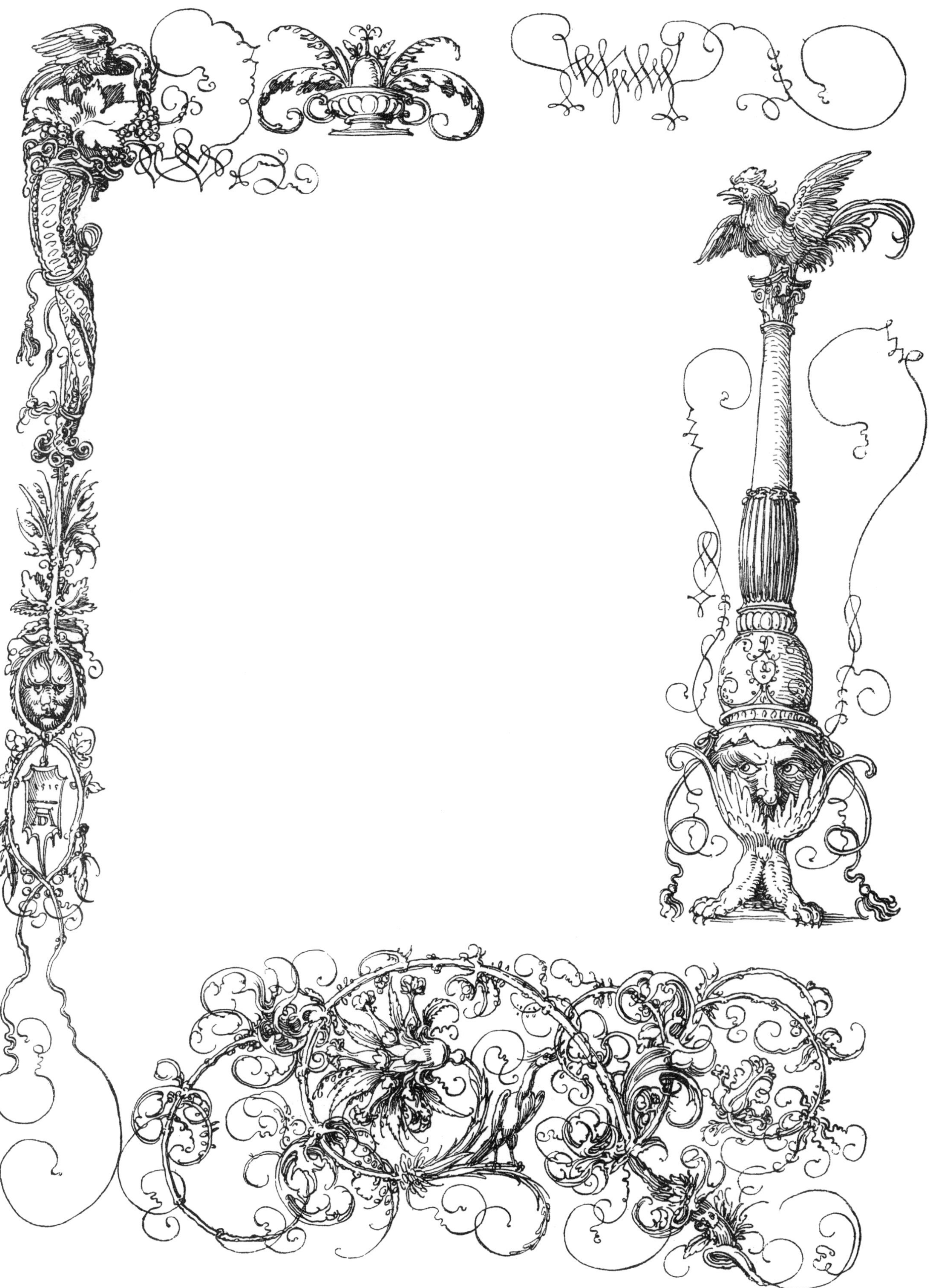

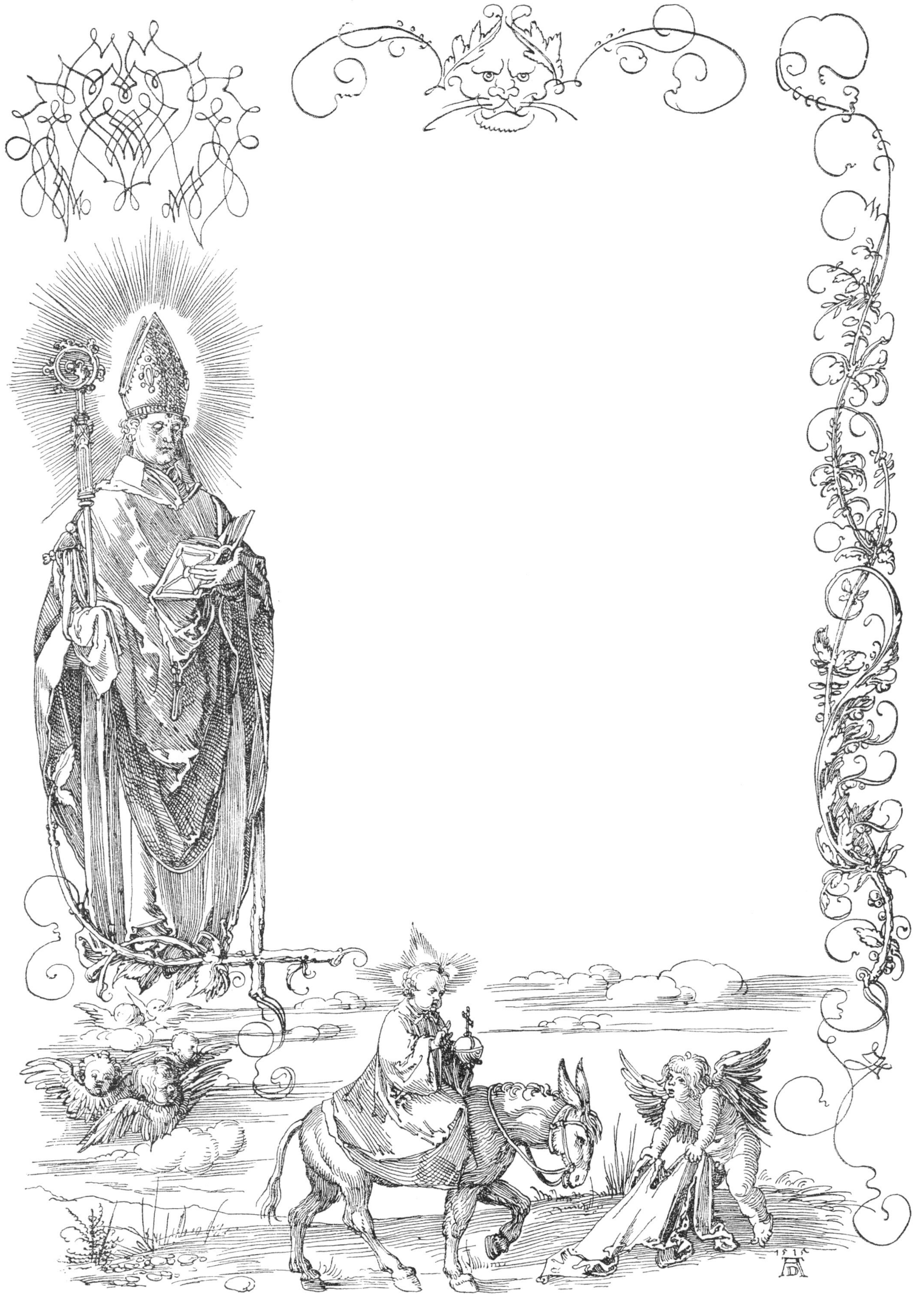

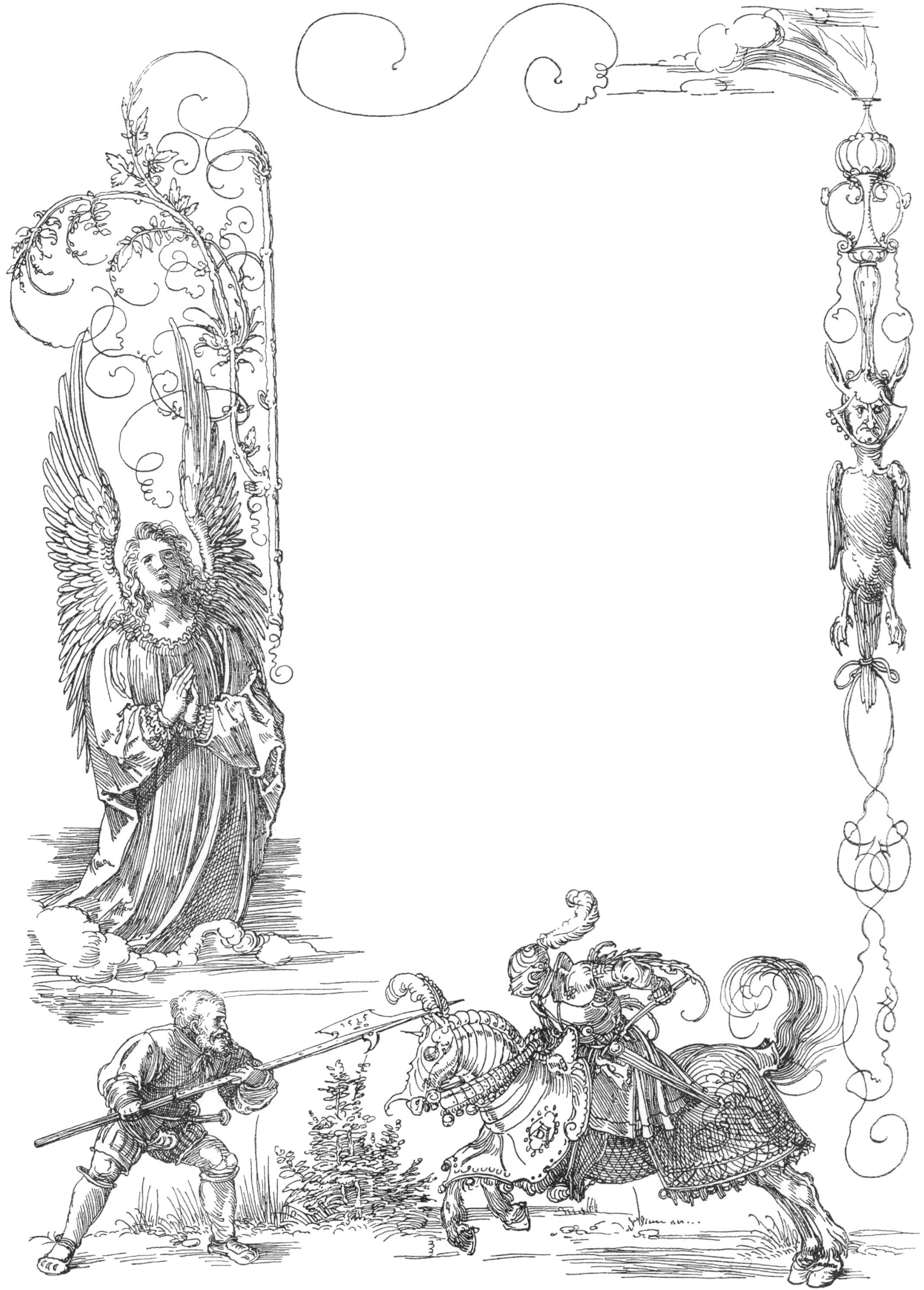

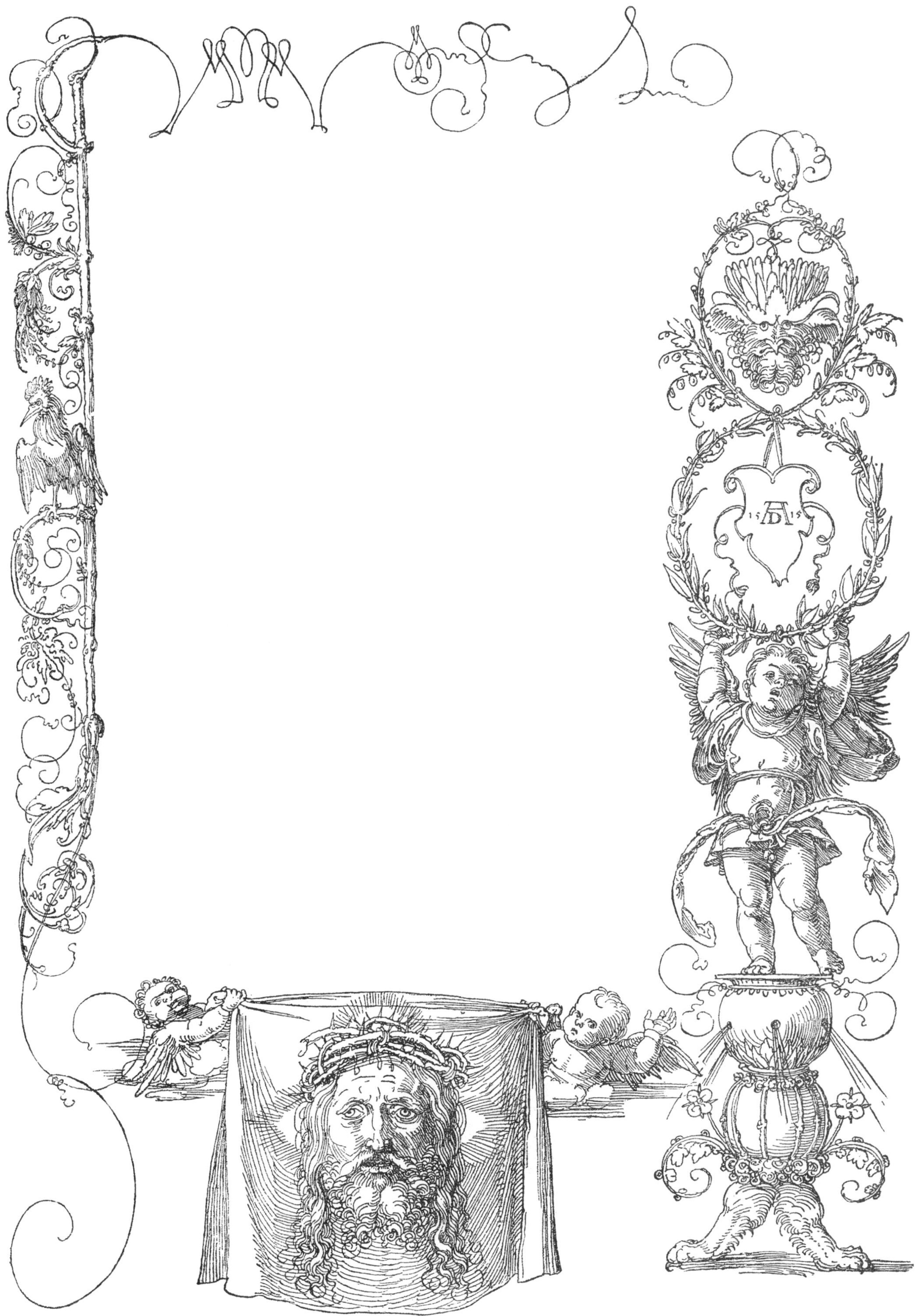

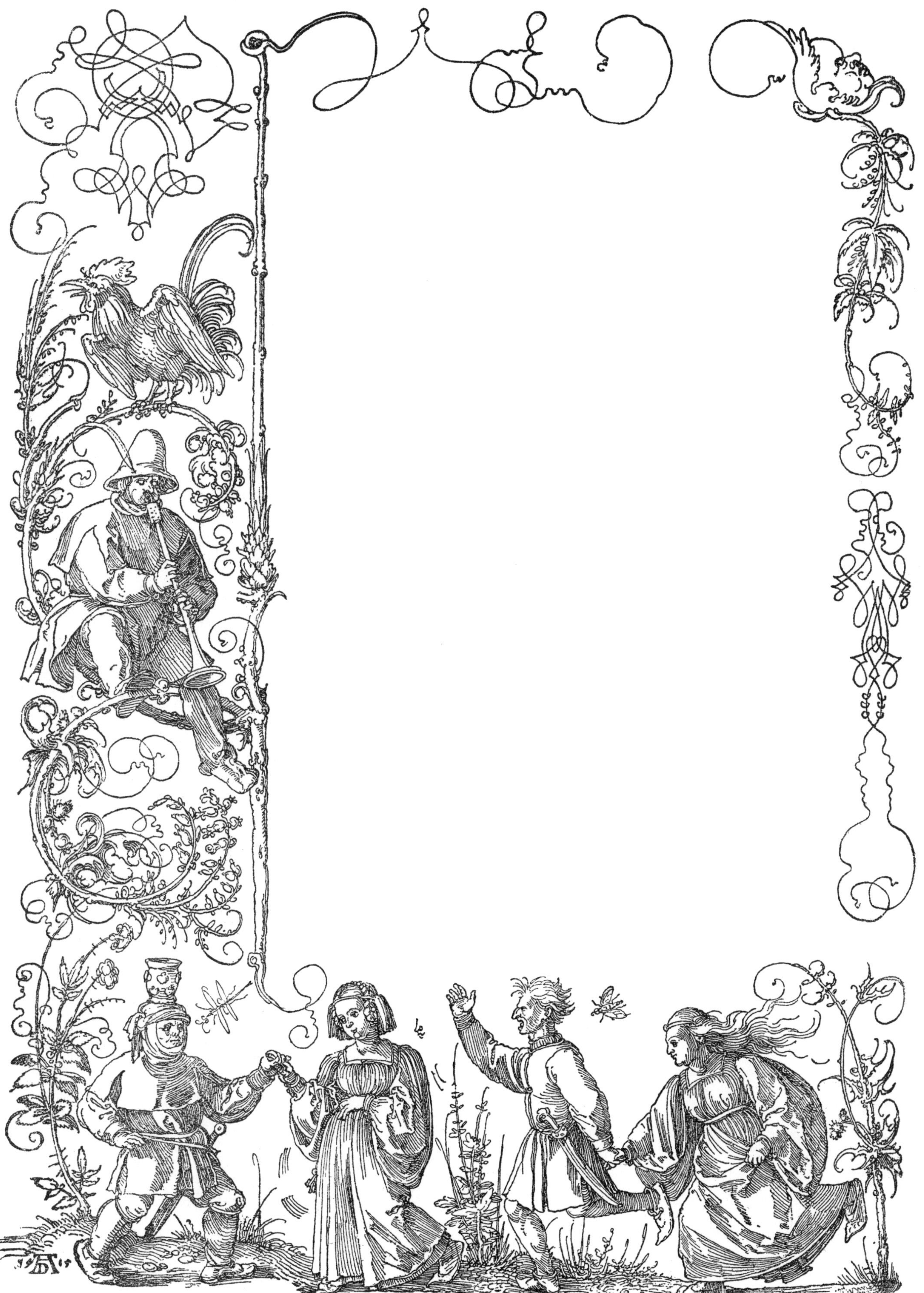

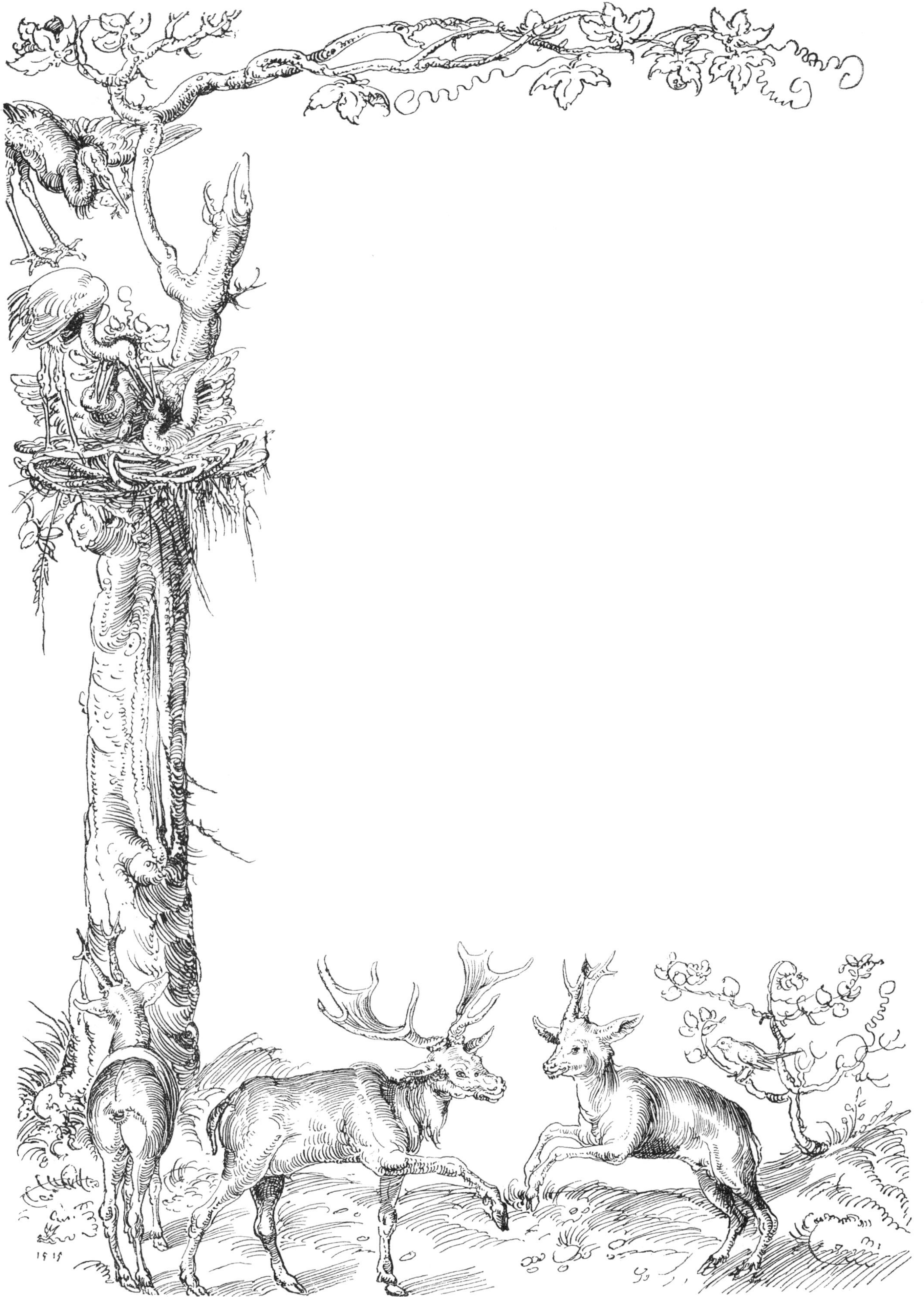

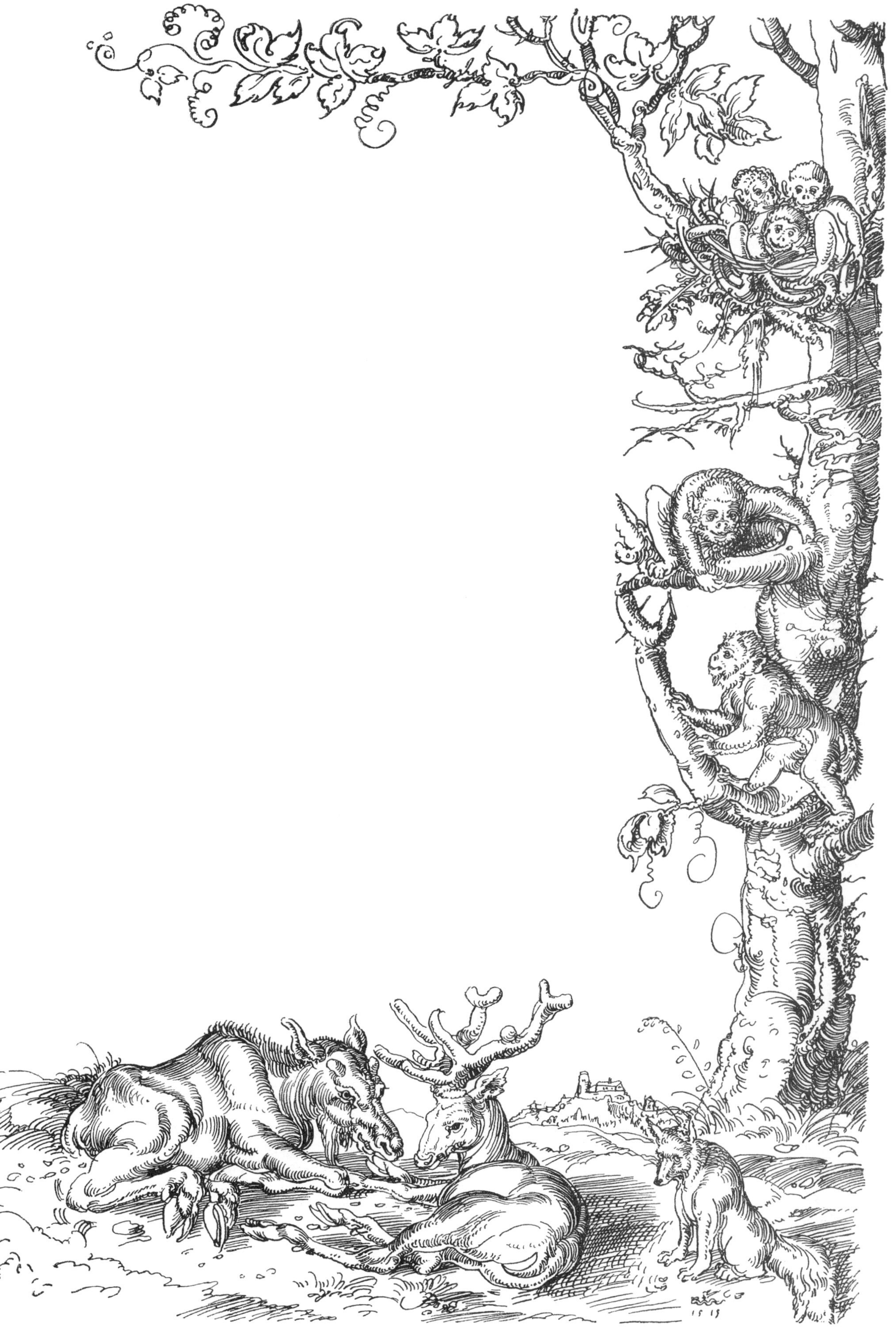

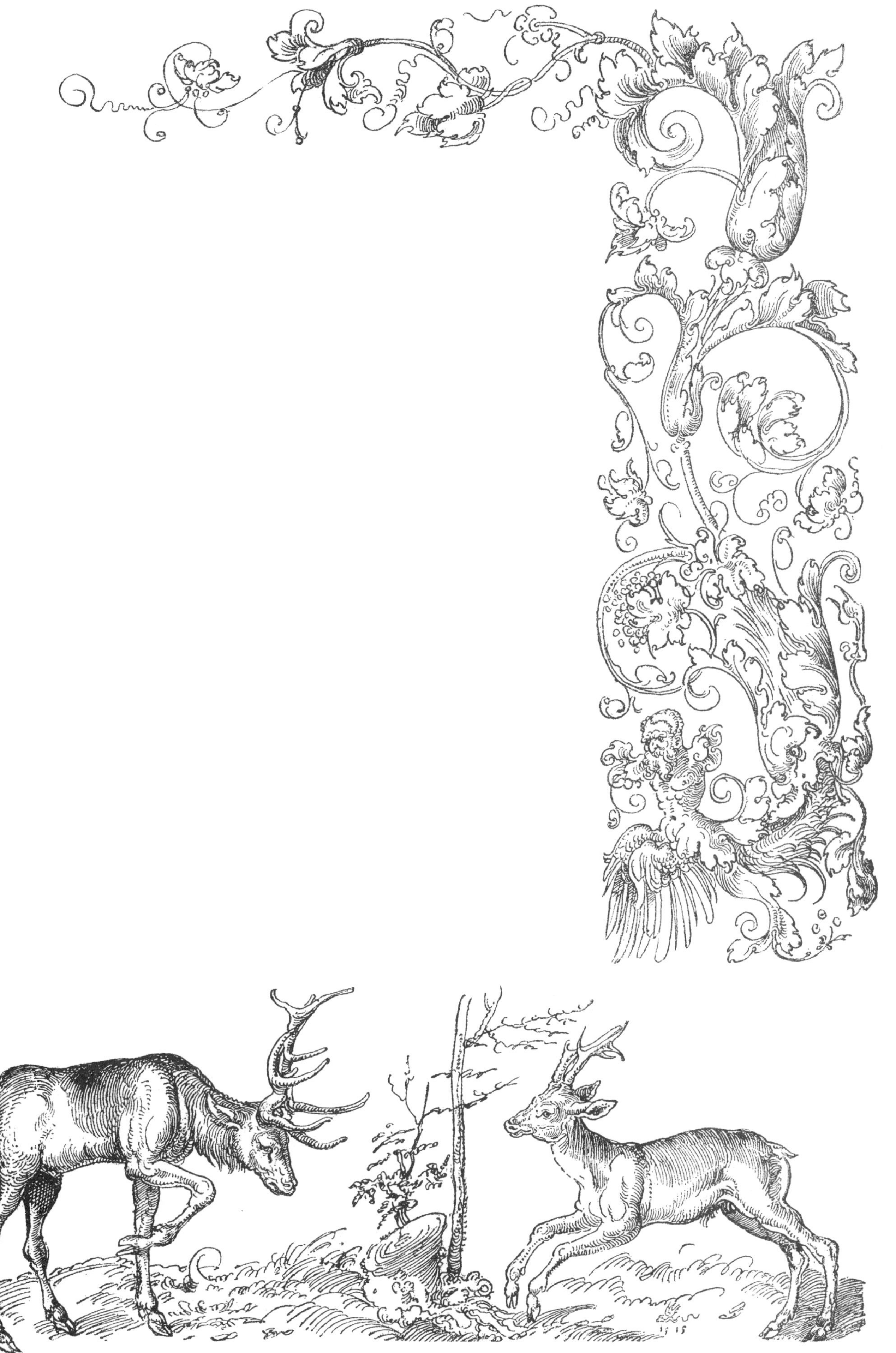

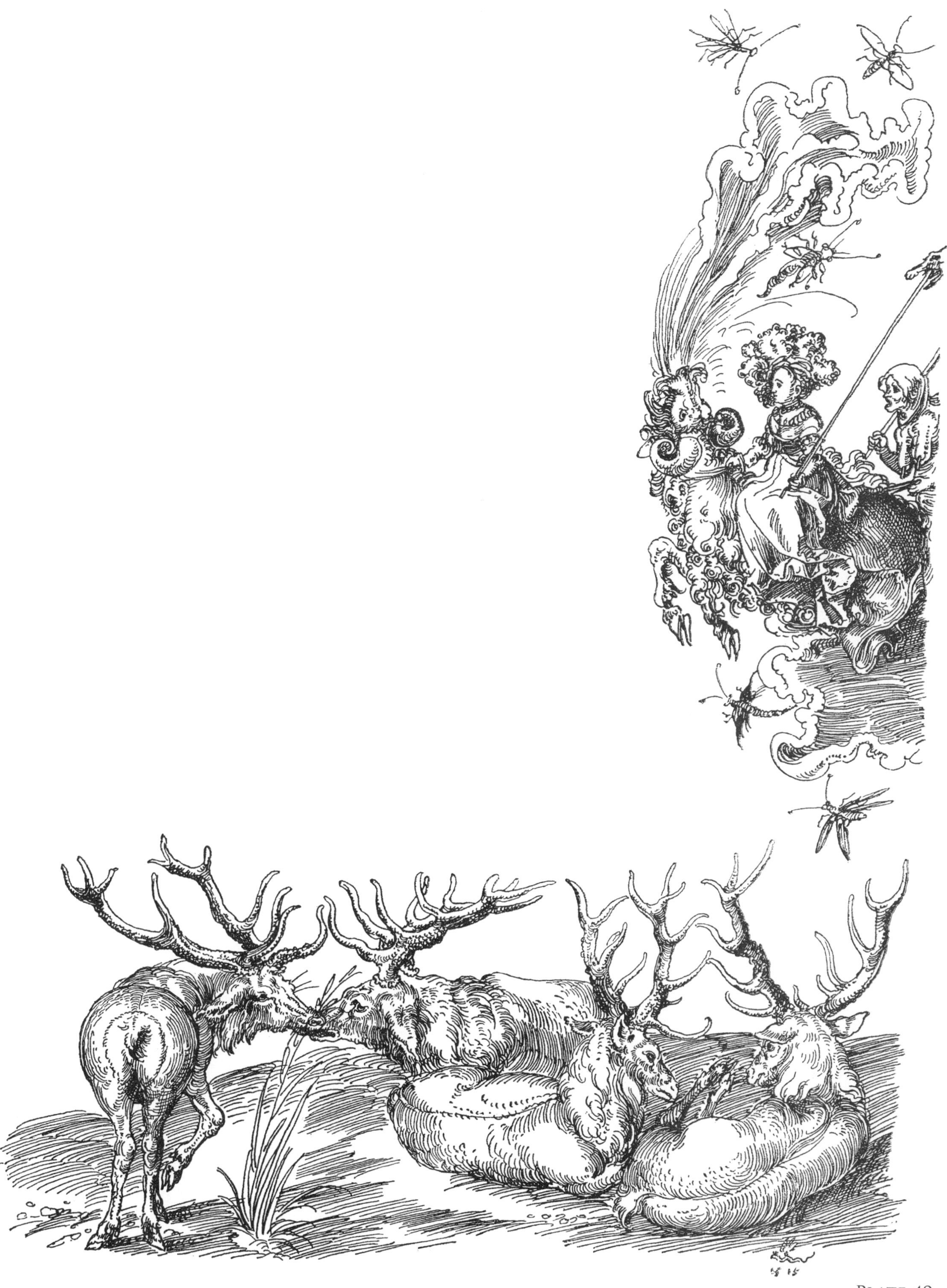

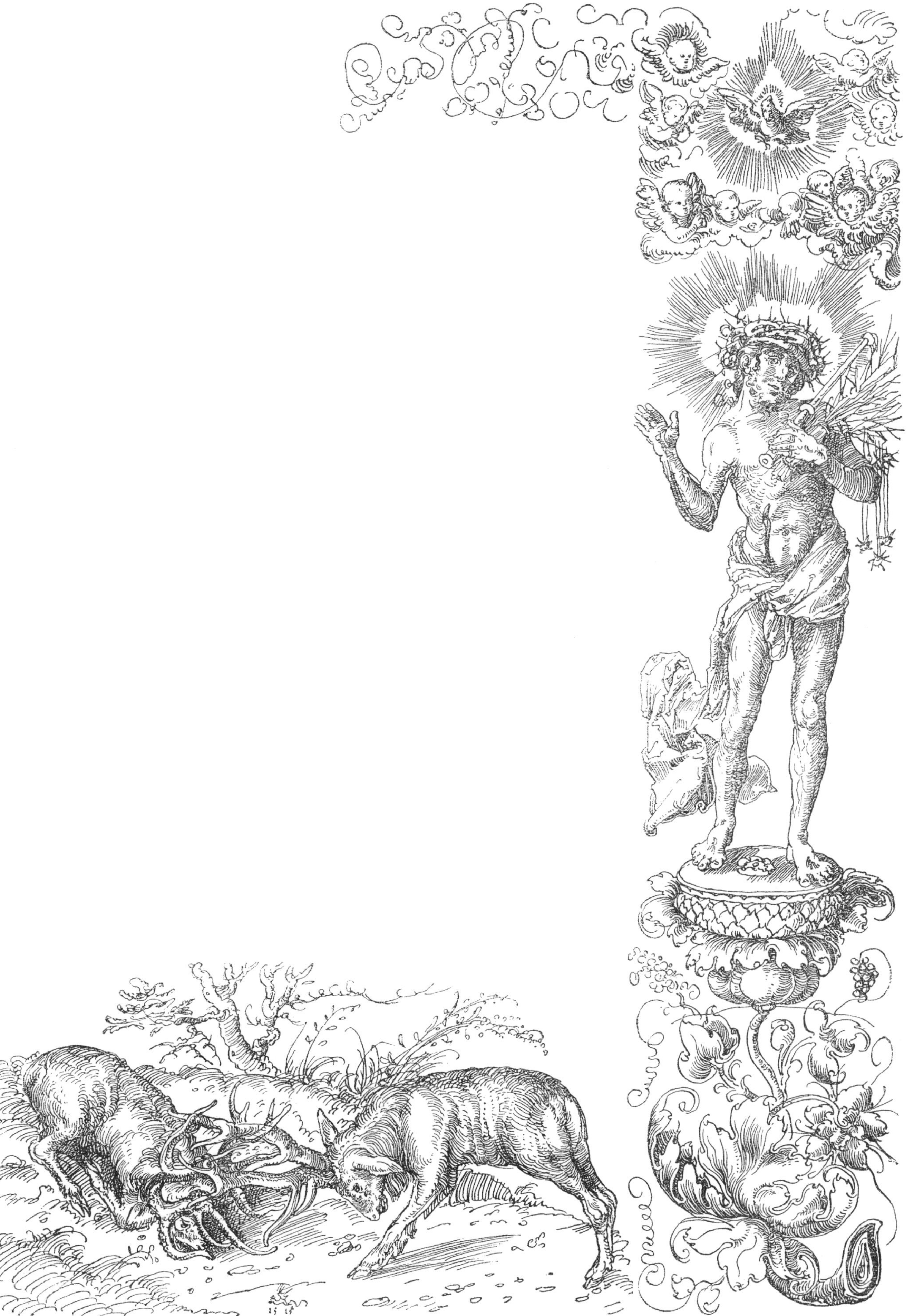

PLATE 50

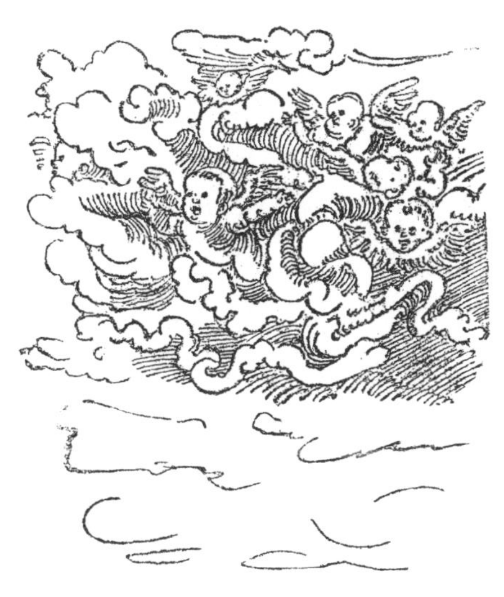

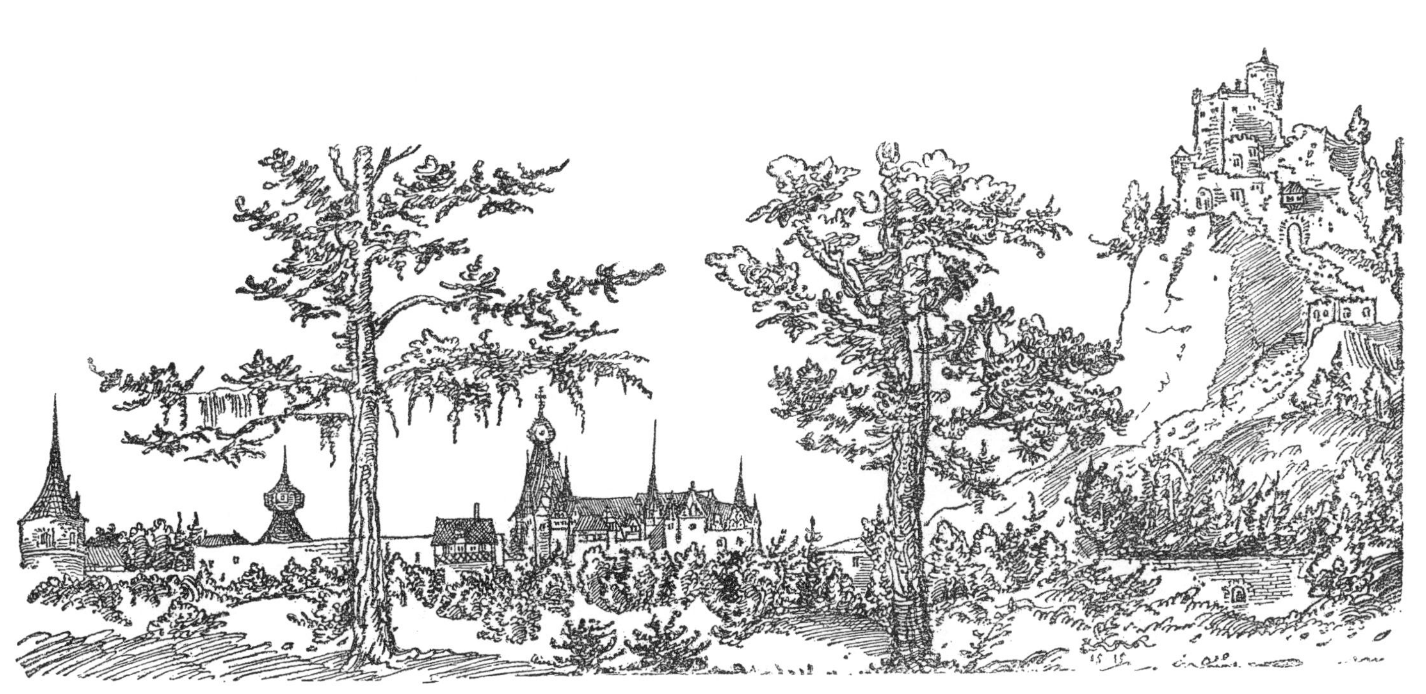

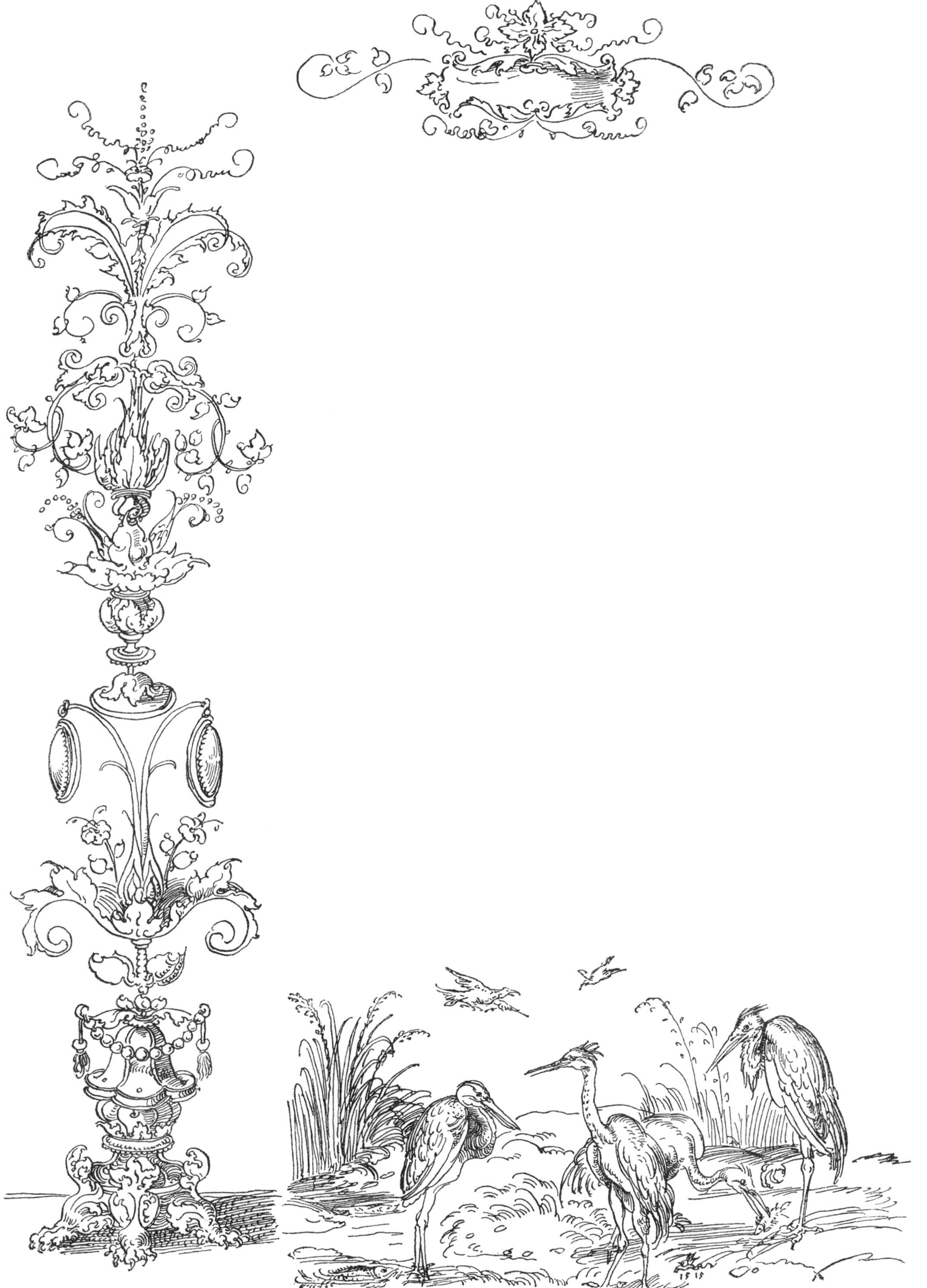

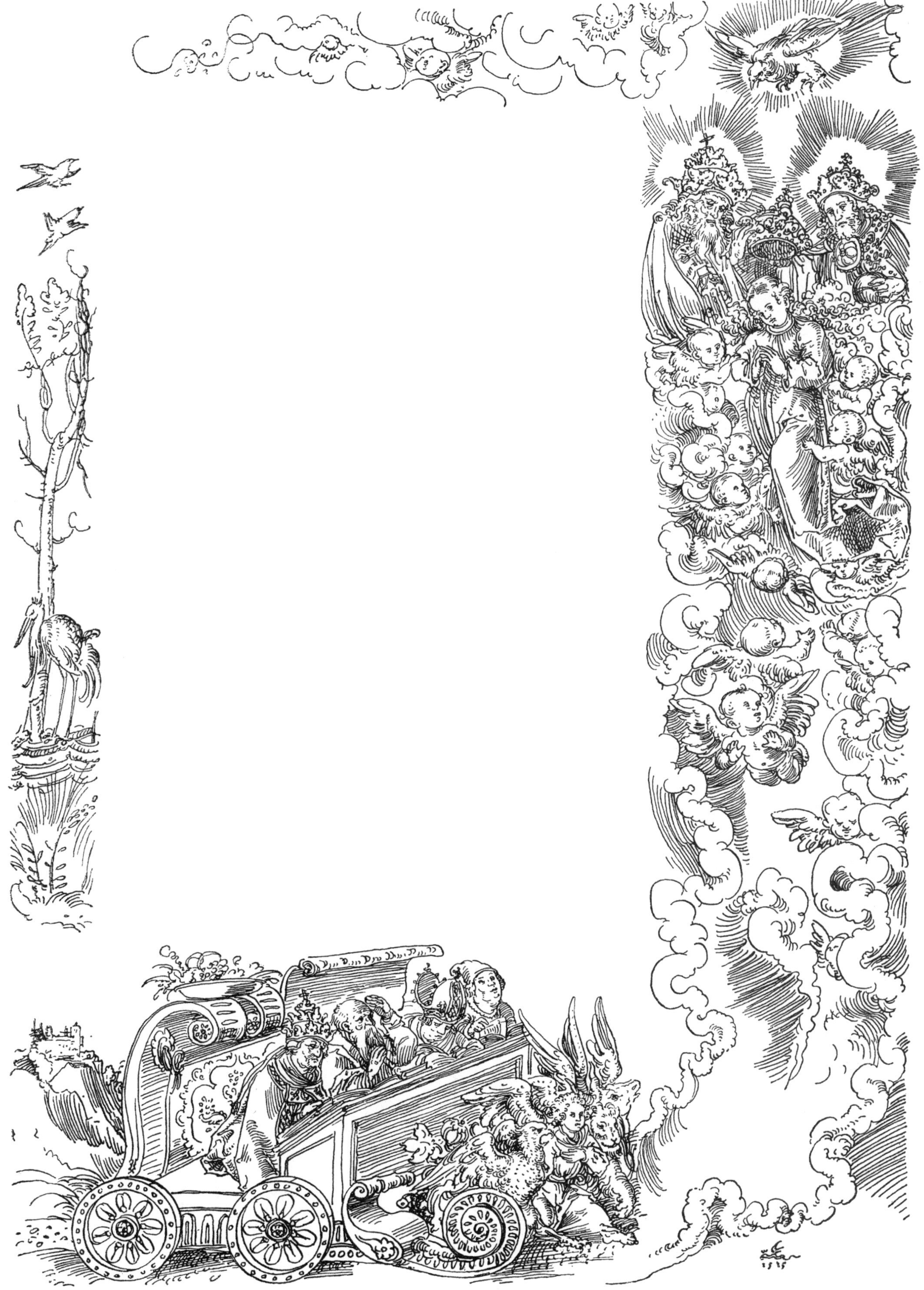